Clairvoyant Wordsworth

Clairvoyant Wordsworth

A Case Study in Heresy and Critical Prejudice

Robert Zimmer

Writers Club Press
San Jose New York Lincoln Shanghai

Clairvoyant Wordsworth
A Case Study in Heresy and Critical Prejudice

Writers Club Press
an imprint of iUniverse, Inc.

For information address:
iUniverse, Inc.
5220 S. 16th St., Suite 200
Lincoln, NE 68512
www.iuniverse.com

ISBN: 0-595-22444-X

Printed in the United States of America

For Richard Hoffpauir,

Who made a scholar out of me.

Contents

Foreword

Much time has passed since the ideas presented in this book first took root in my mind. They have developed through several incarnations: a ten-page paper, a Master's thesis, and now a monograph. In this final form, they have rested idly for years while I sought a publisher. As anyone familiar with the publisher that I finally found will gather, neither commercial nor academic presses were interested. Even the fairly incontrovertible first chapter, presented in essay form to several journals, was never accepted (it will, however, appear in the Temenos Academy Review, Spring 2002). The easiest explanation for this (one might smugly suggest) is that I am simply not much of a scholar or writer. I would be able to accept such an evaluation. However, other reasons for the lack of interest seem to me far more credible.

Neither the ideas presented here nor the critical approach taken are very fashionable in contemporary universities. I am concerned here with determining what a canonized author thought. This may not seem unusual to undergraduate readers, who are still asked to undertake such inquiries in their courses, but those in graduate school and beyond may find this an outmoded, sophomoric practice. A number of reasons could be adduced for such a judgment, but the real reason is, I suspect, as simple as it is unfounded: literary scholars believe we already know what all those canonized authors thought—hence we must turn our critical faculties to other things. I have no doubt that this is an accurate assessment in some cases. In the case of William Wordsworth, however, it is not.

I have often found that critics want to turn long-dead writers into mouthpieces or whipping boys in the service of some contemporary theory or ideology with which the critic agrees. I must confess to having my own interests here; my metaphysical beliefs show through in these pages;

but I hope to make it clear that I have not pressed Wordsworth's words into my service. Rather, I find Wordsworth stating, more or less plainly, exactly the same beliefs.

I hope that this slim volume will reach a few open-minded readers in spite of its lack of academic press endorsement. In particular, I hope to reach those for whom the study of literature—and the study of Wordsworth in particular—might be spoiled by critics and professors like the ones I attack in later chapters.

Robert Zimmer
April 2002

Acknowledgements

I am indebted to Dr. Mark Jones for supervising the thesis on which this book is based, for meticulously proofreading citations, and for providing me with a grindstone on which to sharpen my argument. I also wish to express my gratitude for the financial support I received from Queen's University while working on that thesis.

Introduction

In "Romantic Poetry: Why and Wherefore?" Stuart Curran assures us that the days when William Wordsworth could be "queried about his beliefs in reincarnation in the 'Intimations Ode'" are long gone, "with all their nostalgic innocence" (232). It is curious, and probably a mere oversight, that Curran says "reincarnation" here instead of "pre-existence"; in Wordsworth's apology for the Ode, dictated to Isabella Fenwick in 1843, the poet explains that he did not mean to "inculcate" belief in "a prior state of existence," a state he acknowledges as "an ingredient in Platonic philosophy" (*PW* 4.464). The poet does not mention reincarnation, and commentary on the "Ode: Intimations of Immortality from Recollections of Early Childhood" addresses the issue of pre-existence in the poem, not reincarnation. But Curran's misnomer reminds us that in Platonic philosophy, pre-existence is not really distinguishable from reincarnation. In the *Phaedo*, where immortality and rebirth become central topics, Socrates avers that "there really is such a thing as coming to life again, living people *are* born from the dead, and the souls of the dead exist" (72d-e). To speak of Platonic pre-existence, then, is to suppress Platonic reincarnation: to suppress the passages of Plato least amenable to the orthodox Christian doctrine of the Last Judgment, in which the soul is reunited with the *one* body in which it lived. I shall nonetheless speak of pre-existence in this study even when I discover references to reincarnation in Wordsworth, not only because Wordsworth and his commentators refer to pre-existence, but because it is a convenient and constant reminder that beliefs in reincarnation *and* pre-existence are often suppressed even as they are spoken about.

Is it possible that Wordsworth suppressed his belief in pre-existence? Like Curran, most commentators are sure Wordsworth did not; they accept the poet's explanation for the notion's appearance in the Immortality Ode: "I took hold of the notion of pre-existence as having sufficient foundation in humanity for authorizing me to make for my purpose the best use of it I could as a Poet" (*PW* 4.464). This retraction, most would agree, is sufficient to cancel out the poet's statement in the Ode, "Our birth is but a sleep and a forgetting" (58). Many appear to assume that it is also sufficient to cancel out Wordsworth's references to pre-existence in *The Prelude*, of which there are several, and the allusion to reincarnation in the first of the Essays upon Epitaphs—even though Wordsworth does not repudiate these anywhere else. But the Fenwick note trivializes these references to pre-existence only if we accept as gospel the protestations Wordsworth makes in it. This I am not willing to accept; I take the Fenwick note to be a ruse, a palliative for the orthodox "pious persons" Wordsworth mentions in his apology (*PW* 4.464), and my study proceeds from this postulate. Taking his references to pre-existence as serious statements of belief, I have found—and shall try to help the reader find—that this approach makes the Immortality Ode, and Wordsworth's poetry in general, far less problematic for interpretation.

I also take pre-existence itself seriously in this study, and treat it as a theological postulate as valid as resurrection is in Christian theology. This, I believe, has rarely if ever been done in literary criticism on the Immortality Ode. Such a deficiency would astound us were it found in criticism of mainstream Christian literature; and what kind of commentary on Milton, for example, would develop if no Christian had ever read him? If we read literature from a foreign culture with foreign religious ideas, would we not consider it a gross deficiency if we failed to engage the criticism arising from within this foreign milieu? If, as I propose, Wordsworth took pre-existence seriously, this study addresses a deficiency of this order. Furthermore, the study becomes a reconstruction of the way Victorian readers unfamiliar with Wordsworth's recantations, and sympathetic to pre-existence, might have read the Ode. As I show in chapter four, I read the Ode much as Elizabeth Barrett Browning read it.

Ancillary to the issue of pre-existence is the issue of the peculiar perceptions of the natural world that Wordsworth describes in *The Prelude* and decries the loss of in the Ode. Since the loss of these prompts the introduction of pre-existence in the Ode, I aim to define these perceptions in hopes of clarifying the source of the confidence with which the poet announces that "Our birth is but a sleep and a forgetting." In the process of these clarificatory efforts, I discuss a number of passages from *The Prelude*, "Tintern Abbey," and the lines "Composed upon an Evening of Extraordinary Splendour and Beauty." I argue that these passages indicate Wordsworth's possession, or at least his claims to the possession, of a faculty of supersensible perception distinct from but related to common imagination. Thus, I propose that commentators have generally been mistaken in thinking that the "celestial light" no longer visible in the Ode (line 4) is a universally experienced phenomenon.

Since other writers claim to recall a state of infancy with similar perceptions and intimations of pre-existence, I compare these writers to Wordsworth's experiences and ideas. Although the poems of Henry Vaughan become helpful in this regard, I find the parallels between Wordsworth and Thomas Traherne to be more useful owing to Traherne's greater clarity. Since Traherne's claims bring up the question of whether pre- and perinatal memories are even possible, I introduce the psychological evidence for such memories from the research of David Chamberlain and David Cheek—evidence which, with the support I introduce from the mind-brain theory of John C. Eccles, may help the reader recognize at least the possibility of a pre-existent state also. After attempting to explain the testimony of the poets with the memory theory of Rupert Sheldrake, whom Chamberlain refers to, I turn to the research and biography of Rudolf Steiner. Steiner, who presents information about supersensible worlds with scientific clarity, is helpful in explaining the relationship between intimations of pre-existence and spiritual perceptions.

The findings of these researchers will no doubt strike many readers as pseudoscience, yet even these readers will have to admit the consistency of the researchers' and poets' disparate claims. This consistency is very useful in clarifying the statements and imagery in the Immortality Ode. More importantly, however, is the conclusion that those open to a spiritual conception of reality must draw from the evidence presented here: there is a life before birth, and some people can remember it. Wordsworth remembered his.

Wordsworth scholars will find here a key to passages in the Ode that have never been satisfactorily explained. Students of Rudolf Steiner will find here remarkable parallels to his teachings about the spiritual world, both in the work of Wordsworth and in the testimony of Traherne and others.

Beginning in chapter five, I examine the critical prejudices that have, since the appearance of Coleridge's *Biographia Literaria* (1817), disabled the kind of reading I develop. I show that Wordsworth's almost unquestioned disavowal of pre-existence in the Fenwick note is only part of the reason critics elide or forcefully translate the doctrine. In the criticism of Coleridge, John Mathison, David Rogers, and Gerald Solomon, I trace the effects of religious prejudice on the treatment of pre-existence; I make examples of John Stuart Mill, Leslie Stephen, Edward Proffitt, and Lionel Trilling as critics who bring positivist prejudices to the Ode; and I show how an assortment of what I call postmodern prejudices against pre-existence vitiates the readings of Marjorie Levinson, Jeffrey Robinson, Gene Ruoff, Geoffrey Hartman, and Fred Hoerner. My taking on the entire critical history surrounding the Immortality Ode in this way may strike the reader as quixotic at first, but I think this procedure is necessary to show how nineteenth- and twentieth-century literary criticism, at least when confronted with pre-existence, is as concerned with suppressing heterodoxy as the early Christian church was.

Chapter 1

Taking Pre-existence Seriously

And wrong thoughts make poor poems.
—Elizabeth Barrett Browning, *Aurora Leigh* 5.165

It is almost universally accepted that Wordsworth never took seriously the notion of the soul's existence before birth. As Fred Hoerner puts it in a recent essay, pre-existence is a mere "chestnut" of Platonic philosophy that Wordsworth "regarded rather pragmatically" (634). This view appears to be justified by the poet's remarks in the note on the Immortality Ode, dictated to Isabella Fenwick in 1843:

> I think it right to protest against a conclusion, which has given pain to some good and pious persons, that I meant to inculcate such a belief.... Having to wield some of [my mind's] elements when I was compelled to write this Poem on the 'Immortality of the Soul', I took hold of the notion of pre-existence as having sufficient foundation in

1

humanity for authorizing me to make for my purpose the best use of
it I could as a Poet. (*Poetical Works* 4.464)

Almost all commentators on the Immortality Ode begin with this tes-
tament in mind, and even those who find Wordsworth's protestations
unconvincing will often undercut the importance of pre-existence in some
other way. H. W. Garrod, for example, writing in 1927, finds nothing to
suggest that Wordsworth "entertained the doctrine otherwise than seriously"; but then he deters us from exploring it as an important doctrine
since Wordsworth is a "sensationalist" and pre-existence is to him "not a
theory of knowledge, but a romance of sensation" (Garrod 117-18)—that
is, it is an irrational idea coming from an irrational poet, and not worthy
of rational explication. More recently (1986), Anya Taylor asserts that pre-
existence must have been taken seriously by Wordsworth, since it is essential to the Ode's intimation of immortality. But even Taylor diverts our
attention from the doctrine's significance when she connects it to the
child's general yearning for "his true mother eternity," a yearning "more
important" as proof of an immortal future than of an immortal past (635).
The only commentator willing to credit Wordsworth with belief is Ernst
Lehrs, who insists that the poet is serious when he writes "Our birth is but
a sleep and a forgetting"; but Lehrs mentions the poem cursorily, and in a
book that does not try to address literary scholars (*Man or Matter*).

I agree with Lehrs, Taylor, and Garrod insofar as they claim that
Wordsworth must have taken pre-existence seriously, but I foresee obvious
objections to such a position. First, the poem may not really be about
immortality or pre-existence at all, despite its pretensions: Wordsworth's
original title was simply "Ode," and his revised title of 1815—"Ode:
Intimations of Immortality from Recollections of Early Childhood"—
may reflect his own miscontrual of an earlier work in which pre-existence
was not an important theme, and certainly not a consolatory theme. This
argument has, in fact, been advanced by several commentators.[1] Second,
we cannot simply ignore the Fenwick note, where the poet tells us that he

merely "took hold" of the notion of pre-existence to "make for [his] purpose the best use of it [he] could as a Poet."

Now, one might argue (along New Critical lines) that extrinsic information such as Wordsworth's later statements is irrelevant to the evaluation and interpretation of the poem;[2] it is useful only to commentators trying to fathom Wordsworth the man, for better or for worse. In this case, pre-existence would be an inextricable theme whether the poet wanted it to be or not. But even a critic using such an approach must admit that the implications of the Fenwick note have become an inextricable part of the poem. As Peter Manning asks, "who now can read the poem without an intervening consciousness of the poet's own glosses on his work, those later simulacra of its meaning...?" (83). I think we have to read the Ode with these glosses in mind, but we should question whether Wordsworth's 1843 description of his poem and its 1804 genesis is perfectly reliable; and, furthermore, whether he convincingly separates using a pre-existence "as a Poet" from entertaining it as a believer. We should also question whether it is really only the Fenwick note we are following when we accept Wordsworth's recantations, and not Coleridge's assurances in *Biographia Literaria* that we will not "charge Mr. Wordsworth with believing the Platonic pre-existence" if we read the poem with sufficient subtlety.[3] These and other statements about the poem are particularly important in this case, for they have and will continue to exert a great deal of influence on its interpretation.

Is there any evidence to suggest that the Fenwick Note is unreliable? As the editors of the Norton *Prelude,* Wordworth's autobiographical epic point out, the poet was concerned with re-presenting himself as religiously orthodox in later life: "he became increasingly self-conscious about how such beliefs [i.e. pantheism] might seem to the orthodox. The result is countless little fudgings, insertions of reassuring Christian reference" (524). Yet few commentators suspect in the Fenwick note an attempt to mollify those "good and pious persons" who were pained by the great poet's apparent unorthodoxy—pained, that is, by his roundly asserting that "Our birth is but a sleep and a forgetting" (Ode 58). Thomas Raysor, however, who refers to the Fenwick note merely to argue Wordsworth's consistent belief in immortality, characterizes it as an "evasive apology for the heresy of pre-existence" (865). I think Raysor is right about this, and the guarded tone of the note justifies such a view:

> [H]aving in the Poem regarded [that dream-like vividness and splendour which invest objects of sight in childhood] as presumptive evidence of a prior state of existence, I think it right to protest against a conclusion, which has given pain to some good and pious persons, that I meant to inculcate such a belief. It is far too shadowy a notion to be recommended to faith, as more than an element in our instincts of immortality. (*PW* 4.464)

Wordsworth advertises that he has a motive for minimizing his belief in pre-existence: he wants to appear orthodox for the sake of the "pious persons" troubled by his perculiar poetic statements. We should therefore be sceptical about accepting his statements here as facts.

Were we to judge from the note alone, we might expect the poet to introduce pre-existence cursorily in the poem, as a mere possibility, and perhaps in connection with some classical source such as Plato. What we get, however, is pre-existence as fact, as a matter of personal observation:

> Our birth is but a sleep and a forgetting:
> The Soul that rises with us, our life's Star,
> Hath had elsewhere its setting,
> And cometh from afar....[4]

There are several ways to reconcile these proclamations with Wordsworth's statements in the note. We might read the lines as statements made *in persona*, in which case the supposed autobiographical basis for the poem—averred both in the Fenwick note and in a letter to

Catherine Clarkson[5]—must be ignored. We might take the approach of Richard Hoffpauir and decide that the poet is merely speculating, in which case his assertive tone shows insincerity, poor judgment, and irrationality.[6] We might regard the speaker as hoping to convince *himself* through his assertive monologue, but we would need to find a good reason for his doing this since, as Ruoff points out, the pre-existence passage offers the speaker no consolation "but impedes it" (252). I think the least problematic way to reconcile poem and note is by accepting that Wordsworth is sincere in the poem and never really rejects pre-existence in the note, even while representing himself as orthodox.

Wordsworth does not entirely dismiss the idea of pre-existence in his apology. After pronouncing the doctrine unsuitable "to be recommended to faith," he adds that it is inappropriate only as something "more than an element in our instincts of immortality"; it therefore follows that as an element of these immortal instincts *an inkling of pre-existence is perfectly acceptable*. Furthermore, we might find a clue to his real feelings about the matter in his expression, "it is far too *shadowy* a notion": is it not precisely "Those shadowy recollections" that "Are yet the fountain light of all our day" in the Ode (150-52)? Finally, after conceding that the notion is "too shadowy," he makes a few important qualifications:

> [L]et us bear in mind that, though the idea is not advanced in revelation, there is nothing there to contradict it, and the fall of Man presents an analogy in its favour. Accordingly, a pre-existent state has entered into the popular creeds of many nations; and among all persons acquainted with classic literature, is known as an ingredient in Platonic philosophy. (*PW* 4.464)

Had Wordsworth regarded pre-existence as something merely useful for poetry, it would be odd that he should go to these lengths to defend it. By pointing to the analogy of the "fall of Man," he even suggests the possibility that pre-existence might be reconciled to Christianity, and the reference to Plato implies the doctrine's respectability among philosophers.

These qualifications are not, in themselves, compelling evidence of sincere belief in so heterodox an idea. But a belief in pre-existence and its Wordsworthian corollary (not found in Plato) of the infant's residual communion with its former home—"Heaven lies about us in our infancy" (Ode 66)—these Wordsworth either alludes to or proclaims in several of his other writings as well. *The Prelude* and the first "Essay upon Epitaphs" both introduce pre-existence as a serious postulate, and *The Excursion* and the "Beauteous Evening" sonnet speak of a childhood communion with God that, at least in the Immortality Ode, is closely linked to pre-existence. That these instances are rarely, if ever, remarked in commentary on the Ode indicates the inordinate weight the Fenwick note has come to exert on assumptions about Wordsworth's beliefs.

Pre-existence is implied in several passages of the 1805 *Prelude*, some of which are retained in 1850. The first reference I can detect is, not surprisingly, in the passage on the "infant babe":

> —blest the babe
> Nursed in his mother's arms, the babe who sleeps
> Upon his mother's breast, who, when his soul
> Claims manifest kindred with an earthly soul,
> Doth gather passion from his mother's eye. (2.239-43)[7]

The Norton *Prelude* footnotes these lines with the explanation that the child's soul "forms an evident relationship with the soul of another human being"; what is more important to note, however, is that "his soul" forms a relationship with "an earthly soul," not another earthly soul, as if to imply that his is not earthly. These lines are omitted in 1850—possibly with the intent of making the poem more orthodox—but some of the sense is recuperated in Wordsworth's replacing his promise to trace the "progress of our being" with "our Being's earthly progress" (*1850* 2.234), which suggests our Being's progress may begin before we arrive on earth. Apart from the subtlety with which Wordsworth alludes to pre-existence here, he treats the notion differently from its appearance in the Ode: it is part of his "best conjectures" on human development, and may therefore indicate no serious belief. On the other hand, his statements quickly lose the pretence of conjectures. Forty lines after his speculations about "our being" begin, it becomes clear that by "our being," Wordsworth means to say "my being": he begins to speak of his "infant sensibility" that was in him "[a]ugmented and sustained" (2.285-87). If the whole passage (2.237-304) is a recollection of early childhood, the "conjectures" must carry the authenticating stamp of experience, however inaccurately remembered.

Another, more subtle intimation of a belief in pre-existence might be found in the reference to Empedocles in Book Tenth of the 1805 *Prelude*. In talking about his youthful enthusiasm for Sicily, Wordsworth mentions Empedocles along with Archimedes as among the island's famous figures who remain "like a comfort to [his] grief" (10.1012-14). The comfort of Archimedes we might suppose to be part of the "clear solid evidence" of mathematics that Wordsworth turned to after Godwinism failed him (*Prel.* 10.899-903); but the specific comfort of Empedocles is not immediately clear. It may lie in the Sicilian's teachings on pre-existence:

> Whenever one of those demi-gods, whose lot is long-lasting life, has sinfully defiled his dear limbs with bloodshed, or following strife has sworn a false oath, thrice ten thousand seasons does he wander far from the blessed, being born throughout that time in the forms of all manner of mortal things and changing one baleful path of life for another.... Of these I too am now one, a fugitive from the gods, who put my trust in raving strife. (Quoted in Head 193)

Empedocles's final words here are particularly suited to Wordsworth's case after the vagaries of the French revolution, which Wordsworth recounts in the books prior to his remarks on Sicily. He, too, had put his trust in "raving strife" and felt like a fugitive after leaving France.[8] He may have taken comfort in Empedocles, not only for explaining the suffering of the apparently innocent, but for explaining his own intimations of immortality.

A more explicit suggestion of pre-existence in *The Prelude* appears in Book Fifth, "Books." After yet another affirmation of childhood powers, Wordsworth declines to speculate about their ontogenetic significance:

> Our childhood sits,
> Our simple childhood, sits upon a throne
> That hath more power than all the elements.
> I guess not what this tells of being past,
> Nor what it augurs of the life to come,
> But so it is.... (5.531-36)

Actually, Wordsworth does not really avoid the issue; through *apophasis*, he implies pre-existence by refusing to discuss it: "what" his intuitions say about "being past" is left open, but "being past" is thereby taken for granted (since it is opposed to "life to come" here, I feel justified in assuming that "being past" is pre-existence and not childhood).

This underlying implication is yet more explicit in the figure that appears in the following verse paragraph:

> It might demand a more impassioned strain
> To tell of later pleasures linked to these,
> A tract of the same isthmus which we cross
> In progress from our native continent
> To earth and human life.... (5.558-62)

Apparently to make it clear that he is talking about the changing habitations of the soul, Wordsworth revises the lines slightly in 1850 to read,

"Of the same isthmus, which our spirits cross / In progress from their native continent." The Norton editors make the obvious connection, noting that the "isthmus" is a "strip of land connecting preexistence ('the native continent') to adult participation in the earth and human life"; they seem to miss the import of this, however, when they find it "interesting that his image should derive from Pope" (180 n. 6). In his influential book, "The Eighteenth Century Background," Basil Willey dismisses the isthmus figure by calling it a "'mere' metaphor," as though the matter of the metaphor's suggestion of pre-existence could be elided thus (269); and Gene Ruoff is equally dismissive in judging the figure to "develop from a context of polemical hyperbole" which allows him to read the lines as "decoratively metaphoric" (242). Applying these standards, we might soon be inclined to find every other passage in *The Prelude* to be "decoratively metaphoric"; the absurdity of which raises the question why Ruoff should be so quick to dismiss a positive affirmation of pre-existence (a question I will discuss in chapter 7). Once we overcome the predisposition to dismiss Wordsworth's suggestions of pre-existence, however, the metaphor of the isthmus, from our "native continent / To earth and human life," becomes once again a real metaphor—a vehicle *and* a tenor—and an undeniably sincere indication of the poet's belief in a prior state of existence.

A stumbling block may still exist for readers who think that statements made in verse, even autobiographical verse, need not be accepted as avowals of belief; we might attribute to the statements about pre-existence in the Ode and *The Prelude* what Lionel Trilling calls "a kind of suggestive validity" (143), or some other Orwellian formulation that would divorce art from sincerity. Such impediments to accepting Wordsworth's sincerity about pre-existence may yet be overcome, however, if one examines Wordsworth's first "Essay upon Epitaphs," written in 1810. In this serious prose work we discover Wordsworth implying a belief in not only pre-existence, but also reincarnation. He begins with a familiar analogy:

As, in sailing upon the orb of this planet, a voyage towards the regions where the sun sets, conducts gradually to the quarter where we have been accustomed to behold it come forth at its rising; and, in like manner, a voyage towards the east, the birth-place in our imagination of the morning, leads finally to the quarter where the sun is last seen when he departs from our eyes; so the contemplative Soul, travelling in the direction of mortality, advances to the country of everlasting life; and in like manner, may she continue to explore those cheerful tracts, till she is brought back, for her advantage and benefit, to the land of transitory things—of sorrow and of tears.[9]

When Wordsworth speaks of the travels of the "contemplative Soul," we might suppose him to mean a contemplative thinker travelling in thought, in which case this passage does not suggest reincarnation. But he speaks of this soul as feminine, which distinguishes her from a living thinker travelling in thought; such a generic thinker, for a nineteenth-century male writer, must always be masculine. More importantly, by calling the soul "contemplative," Wordsworth alludes to the traditional distinction of the active and contemplative religious life, exemplified by St. Francis and St. Benedict respectively. "The eternal and unchanging life of the soul in the hereafter consists," according to Christian tradition, in "the loving contemplation or contemplative love" (Gardner 135). Wordsworth implies his familiarity with this tradition when he says that a child is "[a]n inmate of this *active* universe" (*Prel.* 2.266; emphasis Wordsworth's): an inmate, that is, relative to his former *contemplative* freedom.

The statements in "Essay upon Epitaphs," then, constitute a strong reference to pre-existence, and since this passage closely follows another in which Wordsworth explains his convictions about immortality,[10] it is strong evidence of his conviction of pre-existence.

The image of the soul as sojourner, with its spatial mapping of time, is used in the "Essay upon Epitaphs" passage in much the same way as it appears in the Immortality Ode and *The Prelude*. In the Ode, life is a journey inland from the sea of eternity "Which brought us hither" (165); in *The Prelude*, where Wordsworth at one point refers to himself as "a sojourner on earth" (6.62), life is a journey from "our native continent" along the isthmus of youth to adulthood; and in both the essay and the Ode, it is a journey from east to west, even around the globe. Because journeys can be made any number of times, all of these metaphors could express a belief in reincarnation, and all imply the hope, if not the experience, that life may extend beyond the horizon of both death and birth.

One might still object that Wordsworth does not make a positive statement of belief in the "Essay upon Epitaphs." This is true, but we must also bear in mind the possible social repercussions such a heterodox statement might have had. Furthermore, since the essay first appeared in *The Friend*, Wordsworth would have been reluctant to include material displeasing to that publication's editor, Samuel Taylor Coleridge. Wordsworth was undoubtably aware of his friend's contempt for believers in pre-existence, which Coleridge evinces in a notebook entry of 1810—the year "Essay upon Epitaphs" appeared:

> [E]ven among those, who are speculative by profession, a few Phantasts only have troubled themselves with the question of pre-existence.... [C]oncerning pre-existence men in general have neither care nor belief[.] (3.3701)

Just as Wordsworth had a motive for recanting belief in pre-existence, he had a motive for stating this belief equivocally: he wanted to avoid becoming a "phantast" in Coleridge's eyes.

I suppose it is still possible that Wordsworth never seriously believed in pre-existence. But I think there is far too much evidence to the contrary. And were I one of the good and pious bishops who drafted the anathema against Origenism in 553—in which it is written, "If anyone assert the fabulous pre-existence of souls,... let him be anathema" (Head 116)—I think I would have to find Wordsworth guilty of heresy, and arrange to have his writings destroyed; or, if this expedient proved impracticable, I would recommend that all anthologies printing the Immortality Ode must include the Fenwick note as a preface.

Chapter 2

Taking the "Vision Splendid" Seriously

I suspect that one of the main reasons why critics have been so ready to accept Wordsworth's trivialization of pre-existence in the Ode is that they cannot see why he should invoke it in the first place. For Wordsworth introduces pre-existence to explain something for which, it seems, much less problematical explanations are available—the loss of a state of being peculiar to childhood. Ruoff, for example, says of the pre-existence "myth" that "none of this [is] necessary to explain the phenomena which had generated the Ode of 1802"—implying, of course, that Ruoff has ascertained "the phenomena" (233). The answer to Wordsworth's question—"Whither is fled the visionary gleam?"—seems obvious to many critics, beginning with Hazlitt:

[Wordsworth] has very admirably described the vividness of our impressions in youth and childhood, and how "they fade by degrees into the light of common day," and he ascribes the change to the supposition of a pre-existent state, as if our early thoughts were nearer heaven, reflections of former trails of glory, shadows of our past being. This is idle. It is not from the knowledge of the past that the first impressions of things derive their gloss and splendour, but from our ignorance of the future, which fills the void to come with the warmth of our desires, with our gayest hopes, and brightest fancies.... What is it that in youth sheds a dewy light round the evening star? That makes the daisy look so bright?... It is the delight of novelty, and the seeing no end to the pleasure that we fondly believe is still in store for us. (281-82)

Wordsworth would no doubt respond to this with the declaration he makes in the "Essay upon Epitaphs," that anyone who thinks a child's belief in immortality derives from "blank ignorance" must be "forlorn" and "cut off from communication with the best part of his nature" (50-51). But one might also account for the splendour with which natural objects are invested in childhood by ascribing it to healthier sense organs, overactive imagination, incomplete metamorphosis of father-authority into super-ego (as Freud might put it)—any number of reasons that do not carry with them the metaphysical and heretical baggage of pre-existence. What these explanations presuppose, of course, is that what Wordsworth means by "splendour," "glory," and "visionary gleam" is of the same order as what we infer from our own obscure childhood memories. This is clearly the postulate Hazlitt works from, and from which he derives the license to speak of youthful desires that might be quite different from Wordsworth's as though they *must* be identical. But in Wordsworth's descriptions of his visionary experiences, the "gleam" sounds like something extraordinary. Since much of this description occurs in *The Prelude*, and was therefore not available until after Hazlitt's death, we might forgive him for assuming that Wordsworth's experiences were no different from his own; subsequent critics, however, have generally laboured under the same assumption, which, as we shall see, is tenuous at best.

The possibility that Wordsworth's "vision splendid" is something relatively rare in human biography has recently (1983) been suggested by Peter Malekin, and although I agree with Malekin's argument for rarity, I think his characterisation of the visionary experiences as "introvertive mysticism" requires some qualification. Malekin argues that when Wordsworth says, "I communed with all that I saw" (Fenwick note) or "we see into the life of things" ("Tintern Abbey" 48), the poet is in fact describing an "introvertive mystical experience" (Malekin *passim*). Malekin borrows his terminology from W. T. Stace, who provides a definition in *Mysticism and Philosophy*:

> The introvertive mystic...seeks by deliberately shutting off the senses, by obliterating from consciousness the entire multiplicity of sensations, images, and thoughts, to plunge into the depths of his own ego. There, in that darkness and silence, he alleges that he perceives the One,...devoid of any plurality whatever. (62)

Although this might accord with a few passages in Wordsworth, for example in "Tintern Abbey," it is clearly incompatible with many passages from *The Prelude*; Wordsworth's "mystical" experiences generally begin with meditations in external nature and subsequently transfigure that outside world. For example, after returning to the solitude of nature after a period of social distractions, he tells of how he would "spread [his] thoughts" until he felt "Incumbences more awful, visitings/of the upholder," but before this he "looked for universal things, perused / The common countenance of earth and heaven" (3.110-16). Elsewhere, his experience is entirely bound up with the world around him:

> From Nature and her overflowing soul
> I had received so much that all my thoughts
> Were steeped in feeling. I was only then
> Contented when with bliss ineffable
> I felt the sentiment of being spread
> O'er all that moves, and all that seemeth still,
> O'er all that, lost beyond the reach of thought
> And human knowledge, to the human eye
> Invisible, yet liveth to the heart.... (2.416-24)

In this passage, virtually unaltered in 1850, we find Wordsworth "communing," it would seem, with both the visible and the invisible at once; he makes this even clearer a few lines later when he proclaims, "in all things / I saw one life, and felt that it was joy" (2.429-30). This experience is most likely the same as that which we hear about in the Fenwick note: that communion with the external world "as something not apart from, but inherent in [his] own immaterial nature." It seems to me that if we are to label this experience mystical—far too shadowy a term to stand unspecified—it ought to be classed as what Stace calls *extrovertive* mysticism, since the experience accords with this classification.

Generalizing from a number of cases, Stace finds that extrovertive mysticism differs from introvertive in that the temporality and spatiality of sensory things remains apparent in the extrovertive experience, while "[i]n the introvertive type the multiplicity has been wholly obliterated and therefore must be spaceless and timeless."[1] He provides a list of characteristics common to the alleged extrovertive experiences of his examples, from Meister Eckhart to Richard Maurice Bucke. These characteristics include a "feeling of blessedness" before apprehensions of holiness or divinity; a feeling that "All is One," this unity being apprehended as "an inner subjectivity in all things, described variously as life, or consciousness, or a living Presence"; a certainty that the experience is real and not a fancy or hallucination; and paradoxicality. Stace adds that, in addition to all this, there is an element of ineffability in the experience that prevents one from expressing it clearly (79). These characteristics are recognizable in the passages of *The Prelude* I have already cited, and one—the experience of the "living Presence"—is something that Wordsworth refers to quite often.

The term "living Presence" actually appears in the testimony of R. M. Bucke, whom Stace quotes at length. Bucke, a nineteenth-century Canadian psychiatrist and intimate of Walt Whitman's, tells (in third person) of an experience that occurred but once in his entire life, but which changed his worldview permanently:

> He was in a state of quiet, almost passive enjoyment. All at once, without any warning of any kind, he found himself wrapped around as it were by a flame colored cloud. For an instant he thought of fire, some sudden conflagration in the great city, the next he knew that the light was within himself [*sic*]. Directly afterward came upon him a sense of exultation, of immense joyousness accompanied or immediately followed by an intellectual illumination quite impossible to describe.... Among other things, he did not come to believe, he saw and knew that the Cosmos is not dead matter but a living Presence, that the soul of man is immortal.... (Bucke 8)

This is comparable to numerous references to a "Presence" by Wordsworth:

> And I have felt
> A presence that disturbs me with the joy
> Of elevated thoughts.... ("Tintern Abbey" 93-95)

> Thou, over whom thy Immortality
> Broods like the Day, a Master o'er a Slave
> A Presence which is not to be put by.... (Ode 119-21)

> and all
> That I beheld respired with inward meaning.
> Thus much for the one presence, and the life
> Of the great whole…. (*Prelude* 3.128-31)

> The life of Nature, by the God of love
> Inspired—celestial presence ever pure… (*Prelude* 11.99-100)

> Should earth by inward throes be wrenched throughout,
> Or fire be sent from far to wither all
> Her pleasant habitations, and dry up
> Old Ocean in his bed, left singed and bare,
> Yet would the living presence still subsist[.] (*Prelude* 5.29-33)

This last instance thwarts any attempt to read the presence as the equivalent of material nature, or even part of human life as we know it. It is something ideal, eternal, and to *perceive* it would require extraordinary faculties.

Another, more extended discussion of the presence is provided in the "conjectures" on infancy:

> In one beloved presence—nay and more,
> In that most apprehensive habitude
> And those sensations which have been derived
> From this beloved presence—there exists
> A virtue which irradiates and exalts
> All objects through all intercourse of sense. (*Prelude* 2.255-260)

Juxtaposing this passage with lines mentioning the infant's mother, Lionel Trilling identifies the presence with her (146), and the Norton editors agree: "for the child objects are irradiated and exalted by the 'beloved presence' of the mother" (78 n. 7). The case for this, however, relies on the proximity of "presence" and "mother" in the 1850 version, where they appear in succession: "[The Babe] with his soul / Drinks in the feelings of his Mother's eye! / For him, in one dear presence, there exists...." (236-39). In 1805, however, they are separated by *thirteen* lines, comprising three end-stops; it is therefore almost impossible to take the mother as the referent of *presence*.[2] Although one might still see in Wordsworth's revisions an effort to connect the two, the absence of an implicated mother in the other appearances of the "presence" ought to raise some doubts about the validity of such a reading; and the persistence of this presence even after the destruction of the world precludes such and identification. I think we would be much less justified in ascribing to Wordsworth anticipations of Freud, as Trilling seems to do by equating mother and presence, than in pronouncing him an extrovertive mystic in Stace's classification.

Stace himself introduces Wordsworth in his discussion of extrovertive mystics but, seeming to confine himself to the evidence of "Tintern Abbey," is reluctant to accord him a place in this category. After quoting lines 95-102, in which Wordsworth tells of his "sense sublime / Of something far more deeply interfused," Stace tries to call the poet's candour into question:

> Plainly [this passage] expresses something essentially the same as what the extrovertive mystics tell us they have experienced. But it is probable that Wordsworth never had such a definite experience.... Mystical ideas have passed from the mystics into the general stream of ideas in history and literature. Sensitive people can acquire them and feel sympathy with them, and can, in the presence of nature, feel in themselves the sort of feelings which Wordsworth here expresses. (81)

Obviously, this argument could apply as well to Stace's other examples—Meister Eckhart, Böhme, Bucke, *et al.* That it is only Wordsworth whom he suspects of imitating other mystics seems to proceed from his following Bucke, whose *Cosmic Consciousness* is the source for many of Stace's examples. Bucke points out that early on in "Tintern Abbey," Wordsworth seems to doubt his experience with the words, "If this / Be but a vain belief" (50-51); and doubt does not accord with that feeling of certainty both Bucke and Stace expect from genuine mystics.

Besides the obvious inadequacy of restricting their judgment to "Tintern Abbey," Stace and Bucke fail to see a possibility of reading the lines in such a way that Wordsworth's certainty about the experience itself is recuperated—a failure in no way peculiar to them. It is not, I believe, his ability to "see into the life of things" that is called into question (Wordsworth is quite certain about this elsewhere), but rather the idea that this ability arises from the influence of the "beauteous forms" the poet is addressing.[3] There is no reason why we cannot, therefore, classify Wordsworth as an extrovertive mystic using Stace's classification.

The taxonomy of mysticism developed by Stace is, I believe, helpful in establishing the peculiarity of those experiences of Wordsworth's that Hazlitt wanted to reduce to a common "romantic enthusiasm of youth" (282). But it is not altogether clear that extrovertive mystics see nature "Apparelled in celestial light," that is, in the lost glory of the Ode, although they share with Wordsworth the perception of a "living Presence" that may make all things appear as though apparelled thus. Because of this uncertainty, I would prefer to characterize Wordsworth as having possessed a *faculty for supersensible perception* (clairvoyance), leaving the question open, whether this is part of, or in addition to, an extrovertive mysticism. This faculty is what I assume Wordsworth to have meant by the "infant sensibility" that was in him "[a]ugmented and sustained" (*Prel.* 2.285-87), and it is what I assume enabled him to perceive the "Presence."

It may be objected that by dubbing a "perception" what might still be regarded as hallucinatory or imaginary, I accord a certain reality to the supersensory impressions perceived through this faculty. The existence of this supersensible realm is a matter of faith, one might say, unless one can see it for oneself. But similar epistemological concerns surround our ideas about prehistory, for example, yet these are discussed in scientific forums as though they were matters of observable fact. In any case, and more important to our interpretation of Wordsworth, we find that the poet himself refers to his perceptions of an objective, supersensible world and presence, almost as though he expected everyone to have perceived these at one time or another. In the Immortality Ode, "the Man perceives ['the vision splendid'] die away, / And fade into the light of common day (76-77); this suggests that the vision, the "glory and the dream," still exists, even though the speaker's failing faculties prevent him from seeing it. As Alan Grob notices, Wordsworth makes it clear that "the splendour" is something that "belongs to the external objects of perception rather than to the internal modes of perceiving" (250).

A case may nevertheless be made that the "visionary gleam" Wordsworth is talking about in the Ode is merely a quality projected onto the external world by something like the poetic faculty, or simply the imagination. This is the argument of Paul Magnuson, for example, who finds an equivalent of the gleam in the "auxiliar light" that Wordsworth says "Came from [his] mind, which on the setting sun / Bestowed new splendour" (*Prel.* 2.387-89; qtd. by Magnuson 27). That the gleam appears to issue from the speaker here becomes complicated, however, when we consider that he may be "unable to think of external things as having external existence" (*PW* 4.463); furthermore, his choice of the "set-ting sun" as an object recalls the "sober colouring" given the clouds at sun-set in the Ode, a projected coloring that is clearly distinguished from the lost splendour (197-98). On the other hand, Magnuson might have pointed to a passage where Wordsworth is being overtly metaphoric in discussing his creative process:

> But I have been discouraged: gleams of light
> Flash often from the east, then disappear,

And mock me with a sky that ripens not
Into a steady morning. (*Prelude* 1.134-37)

Here, "gleams of light" seems to refer to poetic inspiration, and we might be tempted to think that these "gleams" are the same light that the speaker in the Immortality Ode cannot see. Taking this hypothesis further, one could also adduce the "Elegiac Stanzas" on Peele Castle as evidence for a consciously projected light: Wordsworth writes of how he might "add the gleam / The light that never was" to the picture of the castle (lines 14-15). Like the Ode, the "Elegiac Stanzas" speak of "[a] power that is gone," which suggests the common identity of these powers. I think we would be unjustified, however, in thinking that Wordsworth is necessarily writing about the same thing in all these cases. He uses the words "gleam" and "light" in many contexts and may find them part of an apt figure for both supersensible light *and* poetic or imaginative light, especially if he considers these to be somehow related.

Wordsworth appears to explore the nature of this close relationship in Book Thirteenth of *The Prelude*. Imaginative minds, he writes,

build up greatest things
From least suggestions, ever on the watch,
Willing to work and to be wrought upon.
They need not extraordinary calls
To rouze them—in a world of life they live,
By sensible impressions not enthralled,
But quickened, rouzed, and made thereby more fit
To hold communion with the invisible world. (13.98-105)

Here, "the invisible world" (which I equate with the supersensible) is not something the imaginative mind *creates*, but something to which it becomes more receptive. Hence Wordsworth speaks, several lines later, of the "earliest visitations" that were "given" him (124-25)—not projected or imagined by him. The cultivation of the imaginative faculty is necessary, then, to unlock the doors of perception to such visitations; it does not, however, produce the visitor.

If there is any evidence that Wordsworth equates imagination and supersensible perception in his writings, we must consider the definition of "imagination" he is employing before we can assume he means that clairvoyance is reducible to the imagination of common parlance. When he writes of the "visitings of imaginative power" in his early life (*Prel.* 11.252), he may mean something like Coleridge's formulation of the primary imagination as "the living power and prime agent of all human perception… a repetition in the finite mind of the eternal act of creation in the infinite I AM" (*BL* 1.304). Both Coleridge and Wordsworth may be following Berkeley here, for whom all "pictures," which may include supersensible "pictures," are "apprehended by the Imagination alone" (*Works* 2.402); the Imagination apprehends both external and self-generated images. As Alan Grob puts it, Wordsworth sometimes terms "Imagination" that which might be defined as "a suprasensuous reality whose contents can be read by a special human faculty correspondingly liberated from sense" (239). Yet Wordsworth himself is not happy with this term, as is clear from the 1850 emendation to *The Prelude*'s Simplon Pass episode:

> Imagination—here the Power so called
> Through sad incompetence of human speech,
> That awful Power rose from the mind's abyss
> Like an unfathered vapour that enwraps,
> At once, some lonely traveller. (1850 *Prelude* 6.592-96)

His dissatisfaction with having to speak of "the Power" as "Imagination" is commensurate with a man who has had an experience, explained it to others, and was told that it was his imagination that brought it about; whereas he feels it must have been something else, perhaps something for which no word exists in his language. A similar problem of nomenclature occurs in the writings of the clairvoyant scientist Rudolf Steiner, who, as I explain further in chapter 3, refers to explicitly defined *supersensible* impressions as "Imaginations" (*Esoteric Development* 88).

My characterization of Wordsworth's "vision splendid" as supersensible perception is further supported by a poem of 1817 in which the poet's clairvoyance is momentarily *restored*, the lines "Composed upon an Evening of extraordinary Splendour and Beauty" (*PW* 4.10-13). The language of this poem immediately recalls the Immortality Ode: the speaker declares that nothing could bring him "[s]ublimer transport" than the scene before him, "this silent spectacle—the gleam—/ The shadow—and the peace supreme" (lines 18-20). He sees "Far-distant images draw nigh,/ Called forth by wondrous potency / Of beamy radiance" (25-27). He seems to mean by this the radiance of the evening sun, but he declares that another light is also present:

> Thine is the tranquil hour, purpureal Eve!
> But long as god-like wish, or hope divine,
> Informs my spirit, ne'er can I believe
> That this magnificence is wholly thine!
> —From worlds not quickened by the sun
> A portion of the gift is won.... (33-38)

One might still wish to see the "worlds not quickened by the sun" as the worlds of the imagination; but this reading fails when we reach the last stanza, where Wordsworth connects "this magnificence" with the lost splendour bewailed in the Immortality Ode:

> Such hues from their celestial Urn
> Were wont to stream before mine eye,
> Where'er it wandered in the morn
> Of blissful infancy.

This glimpse of glory, why renewed?
Nay, rather speak with gratitude;
For, if a vestige of those gleams
Survived, 'twas only in my dreams.

*   *   *   *

Oh let Thy grace remind me of the light
Full early lost, and fruitlessly deplored;
Which, at this moment, on my waking sight
Appears to shine, by miracle restored;
My soul, though yet confined to earth,
Rejoices in a second birth!
—'Tis past, the visionary splendour fades;
And night approaches with her shades.[4]

It should be clear from this that Wordsworth claims to see something superadded and otherworldly, but not through his own efforts: it "Appears to shine, *by miracle restored.*" That the experience can be so fleeting, so rare, and come to the poet at the age of forty-seven, ought to preclude our reading it as "the romantic enthusiasm of youth" (Hazlitt), "the freshness of all things to [the child's] newly opened sight" (Ruskin), "the Fancy" (Trilling), "unity with the mother" (Ross) or—becoming absurd—"the worldly renewal heralded by the French Revolution" (Levinson).[5] If we wish to see the "visionary splendour" as the product of imagination or the Fancy—imagination distinct from hallucination—we must question whether it is possible for a person to have such sporadic use of it. Could someone have the ability to imagine things one hour, and, while maintaining consciousness, lose this ability entirely the next hour? The brevity and intensity of Wordsworth's experience are, however, perfectly explicable as the sudden restoration of supersensible perception, somehow triggered by a scene of sensible beauty. Since organs for supersensible perception are conceivably analogous to organs for physical perception, we can imagine (and imagine always, if at all!) that their functioning is subject to the same vicissitudes, regardless of conscious attempts to maintain their full operation.

The relationship between scenes of natural beauty and the reactivation of this faculty remains somewhat obscure, as indeed it probably did for Wordsworth. At times, he seems to perceive the "presence" while his physical senses are engaged; elsewhere it is when "the light of sense / Goes out in flashes" that he is shown "The invisible world" (*Prel.* 6.534-36). In another passage he seems to blame "The most despotic of our senses," "the bodily eye" for anaesthetizing him to "Nature, and the spirit of the place" (*Prel.* 11.169-75). He clearly distinguishes between Romantic enthusiasms for nature and the kind of experience he would like to revive:

> Though 'twas a transport of the outward sense,
> Not of the mind—vivid but not profound—
> Yet was I often greedy in the chace,
> And roamed from hill to hill, from rock to rock,
> Still craving combinations of new forms,
> New pleasure, wider empire for the sight,
> Proud of its own endowments, and rejoiced
> To lay the inner faculties asleep. (11.187-94)

This flighty indulgence in Earth's "superficial things" (11.159) echoes the poet's indictment of her in the Immortality Ode, where she makes her "Inmate Man / Forget the glories he hath known" (83-84). It should be clear from the passages in *The Prelude*, however, that this is an attack not so much on Earth, as on a way of looking at her that prevents one from seeing "Nature, by the love of God / Inspired—celestial presence ever pure" (11.99-100).

The genesis of this "earthly" kind of looking (which seems to be bound up with a way of thinking) is, I think, described in the passages on infancy.

The perception of spirit-in-Nature that first endeared the poet to her is suddenly lost, or at least interrupted:

> For now a trouble came into my mind
> From unknown causes: I was left alone
> Seeking the visible world, nor knowing why.   (2.291-93)

The biographical critic might be tempted to see this as the death of Wordsworth's mother, but such a reading is thwarted by the phrase, "From unknown causes": if trouble came into his mind after his mother's death, he would have known exactly what the cause was. It is also incumbent upon us to account for the speaker's "Seeking the visible world": why must anyone "seek" that which is "visible"? This makes sense only if we posit the poet's certainty, that he had formerly communed with an *invisible* world, and that this seemed to have left him alone; he could no longer see and commune with it, and had to seek solace in the visible world. Although the supersensible "presence" no longer endears objects to him by irradiating them, his affections for these objects remain, and he begins to see them with greater definition:

> The props of my affections were removed,
> And yet the building stood, as if sustained
> By its own spirit. All that I beheld
> Was dear to me, and from this cause it came
> That now to Nature's finer influxes
> My mind lay open—to that more exact
> And intimate communion which our hearts
> Maintain with the minuter properties
> Of objects which are already beloved.... (2.294-302)

Here, he seems to be describing the development of discernment, of his ability to analyse the "visible world" into its constituent parts, and to enjoy it for its details. This appears to be the origin of that earthly seeing which eventually becomes "despotic."

Although Wordsworth does not make the connection, it seems to me that the atrophying of his "infant sensibility" is what enables his discernment to develop, as though the energies involved in one kind of perception were diverted into another. From the sounds of this, he is able to recall a very early stage in his development—certainly much earlier than the time of his mother's death, when he was seven—which astounding recall Wordsworth avers when he writes, "the days gone by / Come back upon me from the dawn almost / Of life" (*Prel.* 11.333-35). If we read this literally, we find a claim to an almost unheard of extension of memory, such as we must doubt without corroboration. However uncommon, Wordsworth is not unique in this power of recall; one encounters the ability again in the work of Thomas Traherne, whom I shall discuss at length in chapter 3. Traherne also claims to remember life "from the womb" and to have perceived "Eternity... manifest in the light of day," and he blames the loss of this sense on inurement to social conventions (*Centuries* 153). But for him this involved learning to prize "the strange riches of man's invention" over "the knowledge of Heaven and Earth" (*Centuries* 160), whereas for Wordsworth the loss involved an absorption in all earthly things.

The reason for Wordsworth's recourse to the idea of pre-existence to account for the presence and loss of his faculties may remain somewhat unclear. We do not find a similar belief in a life before birth avowed by R. M. Bucke, for example, who also saw a "living Presence" in his epiphany, although his vision was perhaps too fleeting to induce intimations of immortality; we would no sooner expect a man born blind and blessed with a few moments of sight to gain any understanding of our experience of visual horizons. Philosophical teachers of pre-existence, too, do not provide us with a solid connection of "infant sensibility" and a pre-incarnate state. Although Thomas Taylor finds evidence for pre-existence in the laughter of sleeping infants,[6] neither Plato nor any Neoplatonic writer uses recollected perceptions of childhood to support the doctrine. We must turn to other writers to discover the intimate connections between the "infant sensibility," "visionary gleam," and intimations of pre-existence—connections I will make clear in the next chapter. At this point, I hope to have established that the lost light Wordsworth laments in the Ode is something extraordinary, even though at the age of seventy-three he characterizes it as something to which "every one, if he would look back, could bear testimony" (*PW* 4.463-64). I myself can remember no such thing, and despite the claims of critics like Hazlitt, who think they remember the same light but show no evidence of it, I think there are very few people who can bear testimony to Wordsworth's experience.

Were more of us able to remember "the dawn almost / Of life," I am sure such consciousness would prompt many more of us to speculate as Wordsworth did (if it is mere speculation); our sense of having forgotten infancy would be replaced by a sense of having forgotten a pre-incarnate or prenatal state of existence. I shall consider the argument that Wordsworth might even base his belief on glimmerings of prenatal life, the possibility of which memories are advanced in the modern clinical work of David Chamberlain and others (p. 51-55, below). For now, we shall attempt to corroborate and clarify Wordsworth's recollections by turning to the testimony of other writers who connect unique childhood perceptions with pre-existence, whether *in spiritu* or *in utero*.

Chapter 3

Wordsworth in Context: Vaughan, Traherne, Chamberlain, and Steiner

Transfigured Nature and Pre-existence in Henry Vaughan (1622-1695)

In comparing the poetry of Henry Vaughan with Wordsworth's Immortality Ode, I wish to show how the authors come to similar conclusions about their own genesis, based on similar recollections from childhood. I do not wish to suggest, as some critics have, that Wordsworth was actually influenced by Vaughan. In fact, I wish to dispute whether Wordsworth knew of Vaughan at all, and to suggest thereby the independence, and thus greater veracity, of the self-observations they make in their poems.

The first thorough comparison of the two poets seems to be L. R. Merrill's 1922 article, "Vaughan's Influence upon Wordsworth's Poetry." His claims for influence, and all such claims afterwards, rest almost entirely on the striking similarity between Vaughan's "The Retreat" and the Immortality Ode. One might almost suspect Wordsworth of having plagiarized Vaughan's ideas and expressions:

> Happy those early days! when I
> Shin'd in my Angell-infancy.
> Before I understood this place
> Appointed for my second race,
> Or taught my soul to fancy ought
> But a white, Celestiall thought,
> When yet I had not walkt above
> A mile, or two, from my first love,
> And looking back (at that short space,)
> Could see a glimpse of his bright-face;
> When on some *gilded Cloud*, or *flowre*
> My gazing soul would dwell an houre,
> And in those weaker glories spy
> Shadows of some eternity…. ("The Retreat" 1-14)

It scarcely needs to be pointed out that Wordsworth's theme of lost glory in childhood is much as we find it in Vaughan. Even some of the metaphors are the same: Vaughan's "second race" as the race of earthly life recalls Wordsworth's "Another race hath been, and other palms are won" (Ode 200); Vaughan's spatial metaphor for "looking back" in time is similar to Wordsworth's metaphor, "Though inland far we be / Our Souls have sight of that immortal sea / Which brought us hither" (163-65); and the "shadows of eternity" that Vaughan the child spies in the "weaker glories" of the cloud and flower bear a remarkable resemblance to Wordsworth's "hour / Of splendour in the grass, of glory in the flower" (178-79). For Merrill, it seems impossible that such similarities could be "the accidental result of treating the same subject" (91). Furthermore, he cites an avowal of Archbishop Trench to Grosart, "that among Wordsworth's books there was a much-thumbed copy of Vaughan's poems," which "Grosart verified by consulting a catalogue of the poet's books which were offered for sale, in which he found Vaughan's *Silex Scintillans* listed" (96). Not surprisingly, then, the assumption of influence has become widespread, and is countenanced by as recent a critic as Ruoff.[1]

As June Sturrock points out in a note on the subject, however, there is also good evidence for supposing that Wordsworth was completely unaware of Vaughan, at least prior to 1814 (Sturrock 323). She cites Wordsworth's letter to Robert Anderson of that year, in which a number of English poems are suggested for inclusion in Anderson's *Complete Edition of the Poets of Great Britain*. Although the list includes contemporaries of Vaughan's such as Herbert and More, as well as such obscure names as John Chalkill and Abraham Fraunce, Henry Vaughan is absent. Sturrock takes this as good evidence of Wordsworth's ignorance of Vaughan at that time.

As for the much-thumbed *Silex Scintillans*, there is no reason to believe Wordsworth acquired it any earlier than the year of his death. There is even reason to doubt that he possessed it at all; it does not appear in the Shavers' bibliography, *Wordsworth's Library*, or in Duncan Wu's *Wordsworth's Reading* studies.

Assuming, then, that Wordsworth was not influenced by Vaughan, and in the absence of a common ancestor for both of them (Plato and his school are not a source for connecting "infant sensibility" to pre-existence), I think we should look at "The Retreat" and the "Immortality Ode" as parallel expressions of very similar biographical experiences.[2] Vaughan, like Wordsworth, was able to recall a state of "Angel infancy" in which the "infant sensibility" was "[a]ugmented and sustained" (*Prel.* 2.285-87). Something about this unique recollection was for both of them presumptive of a prior state of existence, the myths surrounding which were available to both of them. By connecting their experience to the myth, they imply—but do not necessarily inculcate, as Wordsworth is at pains to explain—belief in the reality of a pre-existence.

"The Retreat" is somewhat atypical in Vaughan's work, and only a few of his other poems hint at the doctrine of pre-existence. Among these, however, "Vanity of Spirit" (1650) is particularly relevant to our inquiry. This poem may be seen as a further attempt to describe the difficulty of explaining and finding the significance of recollections of a lost light. The speaker begins by leaving his "Cell," where he has been thinking, and begins a meditation in natural surroundings, all the while trying "to know / Who gave the Clouds so brave a bow" (3-4). Subsequently he turns to introspection:

> [I] came at last
> To search my selfe, where I did find
> Traces, and sounds of strange kind.
> Here of this mighty spring, I found some drills,
> With Ecchoes beaten from th' eternall hills;
> Weake beames, and fires flash'd to my sight,
> Like a young East, or Moone-shine night,
> Wich shew'd me in a nook cast by
> A peece of much antiquity,
> With Hyerogliphicks quite dismembred,
> And broken letters scarce remembred.
> I took them up, and (much Joy'd,) went about
> T' unite those peeces, hoping to find out
> The mystery; but this neer done
> That little light I had was gone:
> It griev'd me much. (14-29)

We may find in the gropings for meaning in this passage a parallel for both the ineffability and fugacity of the experience Wordsworth sees fading into the common light of day. The "fires" that "flashed" to Vaughan's sight, like Bucke's sensation of a "flame-coloured cloud,"[3] are fleeting in their illumination; they have become "[w]eake beames," like the embers in stanza 9 of the Immortality Ode. Like Wordsworth, Vaughan recognizes the experience as a repetition of something "of much antiquity." For him, this is expressed not only in terms of diminished light, but also as broken language or ineffectual signification; the "broken letters scarce remembered" point to a time when he was, like the Ode child, able to read the "eternal deep" (Ode 112).

Because Henry Vaughan expresses his intimations of pre-existence and lost childhood clairvoyance in terms much like Wordsworth's, and because there is evidence that Wordsworth was not familiar with Vaughan, it is conceivable that both poets refer to the same experiences. In the absence of a shared discursive tradition that both poets draw from, the correspondences we can see in their poems suggest a specific, genuine experience, howsoever subjective. Unfortunately, Vaughan does not seem to be any more successful than Wordsworth in communicating the original experience; he merely corroborates the sense of loss felt in its absence.

The Meaningful Past of Thomas Traherne (1636?-1674)

In chapter 2, I touched on the similarities between Wordsworth's account of childhood in *The Prelude* and Immortality Ode, and Thomas Traherne's account of how his sense for the spiritual in nature declined. I am certainly not the first to make such a comparison; Bertram Dobell, who in 1903 introduced Traherne's work to the world after it had spent over two centuries in obscurity, was proud to point out how his author anticipated the later poet: "[i]t is hardly too much to say that there is not a thought of any value in Wordsworth's Ode which is not to be found in substance in Traherne" (lxxix). Dobell does not mean to imply that his author actually influenced Wordsworth. He is aware that Traherne, as a poet and an autobiographer, was entirely unknown in the nineteenth century.[4] Dobell sees in the close parallel rather "a testimony to the authentic character of their inspiration" (lxxx). Because of this remarkable similarity, I think it is likely that both writers, with Vaughan, had the same experiences in childhood. Since Traherne appears to recall his infancy with even greater clarity than Wordsworth, however, and since he expresses this more often and in both verse and prose, his work may be used to illuminate obscurities in

Wordsworth. Traherne does not, however, commit himself to the notion of pre-existence, even though one might find many of his recollections presumptive of it; and this is a distinction we shall have to consider.

Fortunately, Traherne left to posterity biographical information in prose that corroborates what he says in his poetry. This is to be found in *Centuries of Meditations*, a series of reflections apparently written for the education of his friend, Susanna Hopton, and unpublished until 1908 (Hayward vii). Like Wordsworth, he begins from the very dawn of life:

> Those pure and virgin apprehensions I had from the womb, and that divine light wherewith I was born are the best unto this day, wherein I can see the Universe. By the Gift of God they attended me into the world, and by His special favour I remember them till now. Verily they seem the greatest gifts His wisdom could bestow, for without them all other gifts had been dead and vain.... Certainly Adam in Paradise had not more sweet and curious apprehensions of the world, than I when I was a child. (151)

The comparison of his "apprehensions" to prelapsarian existence is typical also of Wordsworth, who at one point in *The Prelude* defends his transports by comparing them to "things viewed / By poets of old time, and higher up / By the first men, earth's first inhabitants" (3.151-53).

Traherne elaborates his recollections in "Wonder":

> How like an Angel came I down!
> How Bright are all Things here!
> When first among his Works I did appear
> O how their GLORY me did Crown!
> The World resembled his *Eternitie*
> In which my Soul did Walk;
> And evry Thing that I did see,
> Did with me talk.[5]

One need hardly point out the parallel assertions of Wordsworth, that "Heaven lies about us in our infancy"; or that the light that attended his birth, "the radiance which was once so bright," is even in its obscurity "the fountain light of all our day" (Ode 66; 176; 152). The impression that Nature communicates with the child, so plainly averred in "Wonder," closely anticipates Wordsworth's statement in *The Prelude*: "The earth / And common face of Nature spake to me" (1.614-615).

Traherne clearly thinks of the child as the "best philosopher" as well:

> I was a little stranger, which at my entrance into the world was saluted and surrounded with innumerable joys. My knowledge was Divine. I knew by intuition those things which since my Apostasy, I collected again by the highest reason. (151)

Here we find a parallel of Wordsworth's assertion in the "Essay upon Epitaphs" that revelation (and specifically the doctrine of personal immortality) coincides with the earliest "communications with our internal being," and that it is only through this coincidence that revelation has "a power to affect us" (51-52).

As Dobell points out (lxxxi), the "philosophy" of the infant Traherne bears a remarkable resemblance to that of Berkeley, although, as we might expect, it is not so much reasoned out as it is experienced. He finds in Traherne's poem, "My Spirit," an implied statement of the "non-existence of independent matter" such as Berkeleian philosophy proposes, thus making Traherne "a Berkeleian before Berkeley was born" (lxxxii):

> An Object, if it were before
> My Ey, was by Dame Natures Law,
> Within my Soul. Her Store
> Was all at once within me; all her Treasures
> Were my Immediat and Internal Pleasures,

> Substantial Joys, which did inform my Mind.
>   With all She wrought,
>   My Soul was fraught,
> And evry Object in my Heart a Thought
>   Begot, or was; I could not tell,
>   Whether the Things did there
>   Themselvs appear,
> Which in my Spirit *truly* seemd to dwell;
>   Or whether my conforming Mind
>   Were not even all that therin shind. ("My Spirit" 37-51)[6]

Insofar as Wordsworth's "infant sensibility" and "abyss of idealism" (Fenwick note) replicated this experience, we must call into question speculations that he was strongly influenced by Berkeley. Obviously, a memory of infancy such as Traherne writes of would, for Wordsworth, render exposure to Berkeley superfluous. On the other hand, as Ellen Leyburn shows, it may have been through reading Berkeley that Wordsworth was able to reconcile with orthodox Christianity his view of Nature as interfused with spirit:

> For Berkeley himself the whole value and significance of his system lay in establishing the validity of theism and even, so it seemed to him, of the Christian religion. His *esse est percipi* of the material world led directly in his view, not to scepticism [one might add, solipsism], but to belief in a divine mind constantly perceiving and holding the material world in being.... [I]t would be hard to say that Wordsworth is not following Berkeley completely when he speaks of "Nature's self, which is the breath of God" [*Prel.* 5.222]. (Leyburn 25)

Based on these premises, Leyburn finds both Wordsworth's earlier, pantheist-sounding work and his later poetry "in harmony with the Berkeleian system" (26), and thus thoroughly monotheistic.

Traherne's "My Spirit" is also important for its expressions parallel to the "Soul's immensity" and the "Eye among the blind" of which Wordsworth writes (Ode 110-12). For Traherne, the infant soul is an eye-like "Spirit infinit," as he remembers it:

> O Sacred Mysterie!
> My Soul a Spirit infinit!
> An Image of the Deity!
> A pure Substantial Light!
> That Being Greatest which doth Nothing seem!
> Why twas my All, I nothing did esteem
> But that alone. A Strange Mysterious Sphere!
> A Deep Abyss
> That sees and is
> The only Proper Place of Heavenly Bliss.
> To its Creator tis so near
> In Lov and Excellence
> In Life and Sence,
> In Greatness Worth and Nature; And so Dear;
> In it, without Hyperbole,
> The Son and friend of God we see.
> A Strange Extended Orb of Joy,
> Proceeding from within,
> Which did on evry side convey
> It self, and being nigh of Kin
> To God did evry Way
> Dilate it self even in an Instant, and
> Like an Indivisible Centre Stand
> At once Surrounding all Eternitie. (70-93)

The paradoxical "Centre" that surrounds "all Eternitie" is typical of mystical utterances as observed by Stace (chapter 2, above), and has its parallel in a number of passages in Wordsworth that we have looked at. As for the infant in the Ode, its "Soul's immensity" may be explained in terms of Traherne's feeling that his "Spirit infinit" surrounded all eternity. The Ode-child is an "Eye among the blind" because he sees with what Traherne calls a "Strange Extended Orb," which I take to be an organ for supersensible perception, that can "on evry side convey / It self." The answer to the question, how Wordsworth could so roundly assert such things of children, becomes painfully obvious: by recollections, such as Traherne has, from very early childhood.

Traherne's perception of the relationship between the material and spiritual worlds also appears to match Wordsworth's. For Traherne, things appear alive, perhaps irradiated by some "Presence," which is furthermore perceived as a part of, yet not identical with, the conscious self:

> O Living Orb of Sight!
> Thou which within me art, yet Me! Thou Ey,
> And Temple of his Whole Infinitie!
> O what a World art Thou! a World within!
> All Things appear,
> All Objects are
> Alive in thee! Supersubstancial, Rare,
> Above them selvs, and nigh of Kin
> To those pure Things we find
> In his Great Mind
> Who made the World! tho now Ecclypsed by Sin.
> ("My Spirit" 107-17)

A number of passages from *The Prelude* find their parallel here, and can perhaps be clarified through comparison. For example, Traherne's "Living Orb of Sight" may be taken as the "beloved presence" in Wordsworth that

Trilling mistook for the mother, or as the clairvoyant faculty through which the presence is perceived; as in Traherne, where it makes all things appear "Alive" and "Superstancial," so in *The Prelude* does it "irradiate and exalt[] / All objects through all intercourse of sense" (2.259-260); and through it Wordsworth sees, or at least remembers to have seen, "one life" in "all things"—and he "felt that it was joy" (2.429-30).

After reading "My Spirit," we may begin to understand the ambiguity that Wordsworth appears to express, whether the "gleam" that so irradiates the world in childhood proceeds from himself or exists independent of him. I have argued that Wordsworth generally thinks of the presence as a "visitation," and the fact that he "perceives it die away" into "the light of common day" suggests an independent existence for it. In "My Spirit," however, we find Traherne addressing the "Living Orb of Sight" as "Thou which within me art, yet Me" (108). This subtle sense of otherness within the self is, perhaps, what Wordsworth is trying to express when he writes of having "Two consciousnesses—conscious of myself, / And of some other being" (*Prel.* 2.32-33). The speaking "Me" in "My Spirit" seems to be uncertain whether this "Living Orb" is something apart from his seat of consciousness or if it is, as he elsewhere addresses it, the "Wondrous Self" (103). We appear to be dealing with an identity/division paradox comparable to the relationship between soul and spirit in theosophical writings or higher and lower self in eastern philosophy—not, obviously, to be confused with the Freudian ego-superego or ego-double structures, which can contain neither Traherne's *awareness* of the relationship nor his claims to its existence "from the womb"; in classical psychoanalysis, the superego and double appear well after birth.

Finally, we find expressed in "My Spirit" the feeling that Nature's treasures were Traherne's "Immediat and Internal Pleasures," a sentiment common to Wordsworth. In *The Prelude*, Wordsworth writes how he felt himself in possession of the world:

Unknown, unthought of, yet I was most rich,
I had a world about me—'twas my own,
I made it; for it only lived to me,
And to the God who looked into my mind. (3.141-44)

Wordsworth's is a feeling of private possession, like that of a creator and his private creation; when he says "'twas my own, / I made it," I take him to refer to this feeling of possession rather than actual ownership or creation, a feeling justified in that this world "only lived to [him]." Traherne further articulates such a feeling in *Centuries of Meditations*:

> I seemed as one brought into the Estate of Innocence. All things were spotless and pure and glorious: yea, and infinitely mine, and joyful, and precious.... Is it not strange, that an infant should be heir of the whole World, and see those mysteries which the books of the learned never unfold? (152)

Taking this feeling of ownership as a general premise, we might draw the corollary that an infant feels it belongs to the world as much as the world belongs to it. This sense of belonging is, again, expressed in Wordsworth's observation of the "gravitation and filial bond / Of Nature" that are indigenous to the infant (*Prel.* 2.263-64).

Traherne's case parallels Wordsworth's and Vaughan's in that he, too, saw his faculties atrophy; in his case, however, a subsequent reversal of this process seems to have occurred, which probably accounts for the unmatched clarity of his memories. He provides us with an explanation for the loss of his "infant sensibility" that is remarkably similar to Wordsworth's claims in the Immortality Ode, and worth quoting at length:

> The first Light which shined in my Infancy in its primitive and innocent clarity was totally eclipsed: insomuch that I was fain to learn all again. If you ask me how it was eclipsed? Truly by the

customs and manners of men, which like contrary winds blew it out: by an innumerable company of other objects,... worthless things, that like so many loads of earth and dung did overwhelm and bury it: by the impetuous torrent of wrong desires in all others whom I saw or knew that carried me away and alienated me from it: by a whole sea of other matters and concernments that covered and drowned it: finally by the evil influence of a bad education that did not foster and cherish it. All men's thoughts and words were about other matters. They prized new things which I did not dream of. I was a stranger and unacquainted with them; I was little and reverenced their authority; I was weak, and easily guided by their example: ambitious also, and desirous to approve myself unto them. And finding no one syllable in any man's mouth of those things, by degrees they vanished, my thoughts... were blotted out; and at last all the celestial, great, and stable treasures to which I was born, as wholly forgotten, as if they had never been. (*Centuries* 157)

Comparing this passage with stanzas 5-8 of the Immortality Ode, we discover manifold parallels in both content and expression. Perhaps most striking is Traherne's image of the "worthless things" that bury his "first Light" like "so many loads of earth and dung," which is precisely what Wordsworth predicts will happen to the child:

> Full soon thy Soul shall have her earthly freight,
> And custom lie upon thee with a weight,
> Heavy as frost, and deep almost as life! (127-29)

To Wordsworth's question, why the child is "Thus blindly with [his] blessedness at strife," Traherne provides some good answers—an infant wants to please those around it whom it reverences, and, being impressionable, is "easily guided by their example." Applying this to Wordsworth's complaint, that the child acts "[a]s if his whole vocation / Were endless imitation" (Ode 107-08), we might ascribe his objection not to imitation *per se*, but imitation of the acts and thoughts of those who have themselves lost their supersensible awareness. Furthermore, Traherne thinks of his former self as "ambitious"—not a very sinister attribute in this context, but evocative of the sin that led to the loss of Eden in biblical myth.

Yet Traherne finds that the "Immediat and Internal Pleasures" of "My Spirit" are recoverable, however; in "Ages II," a poem from the recently discovered *Commentaries of Heaven*,[7] he describes a state of blessedness that no longer seems dependent on age, but nonetheless involves an interaction of soul and world that parallels the descriptions we have seen in Wordsworth. In Traherne's terms, "he thats with the Joys of Ages lined" is able to transfigure himself and his surroundings in a way evocative of the Ode-child's powers:

> His Body like a Star in its own Beams
> Environed, a Glorious Splendour streams.
> And sheds a lustre from its own Abode,
> In which it is securd. His Souls abroad.
> And darting evry way in Beams of Light
> That are its Essence tho they seem its Sight,
> Make even his baser Corps a Centre pure.... (85-91)

Again, we find Traherne presenting us with the same kind of curious ambiguity about the location and source of a "lustre" as we found in Wordsworth. In "Ages II," the soul seems to illuminate the world, but this is because it is itself "abroad"; and the "Beams of Light" that seem to facilitate the soul's power of "Sight" are in fact its "Essence," suggesting a kind of communion or intercourse in sight rather than detached observation.

As we did in Wordsworth's case, we might argue that what Traherne is really talking about in his biography is the loss of his common imagination. Whereas such an argument is somewhat difficult to refute for

Wordsworth, Traherne makes it clear that he considers the imagination to be an inferior faculty:

> My soul was only apt and disposed to great things; but souls to souls are like apples to apples, one being rotten rots another. When I began to speak and go, nothing began to be present to me, but what was present to me in their thoughts. Nor was anything present to me any other way, than it was so to them. The glass of imagination was the only mirror, wherein anything was represented or appeared to me. All things were absent which they talked not of. (*Centuries* 159)

Whereas Wordsworth appears to conflate the imagination with his "infant sensibility," Traherne clearly distinguishes "great things" from what he receives through the "glass of imagination" in this passage. This is not, I believe, so much a case of their having different kinds of experiences, however; it is more likely a function of the expanded concept of imagination Wordsworth had, and therefore merely a matter of semantics.

When Traherne says that it is only when he "began to speak and go" that his faculties atrophied, it is clear that he claims to remember a state of pre-linguistic consciousness (even though Nature seemed to *speak* to him). He asserts this directly in a number of instances. He speaks of "pure and virgin apprehensions from the womb" (*Centuries* 151); of how, "before [he] could speak," he dwelt "within a World of Light / Distinct and Seperat from all Mens Sight" ("Dumnesse" 19; 31-32); and, in "The Preparative," of how even "Before [his] Tongue or Cheeks were to [him] shewn," he felt his Soul to be "A Living Endless Ey" (4; 12). Like Wordsworth's "best Philosopher," he is in these poems "deaf and silent," yet can read "the eternal deep" (Ode 111-13).

"The Preparative" implies most strongly that Traherne had some notion of a pre-existence, even though he seems to locate this in the womb. It is nevertheless the site of "apprehensions" of a most otherworldly kind:

My Body being Dead, my Lims unknown;
 Before I skild to prize
 Those living Stars mine Eys,
Before my Tongue or Cheeks were to me shewn,
 Before I knew my Hands were mine,
 Or that my Sinews did my Members joyn,
 When neither Nostril, Foot, nor Ear,
As yet was seen, or felt, or did appear;
 I was within
A House I knew not, newly clothd with Skin.

Then was my Soul my only All to me,
 A Living Endless Ey,
 Just bounded with the Skie
Whose Power, whose Act, whose Essence was to see. (1-14)

Although he feels himself "newly clothd with Skin," he begins by stating that his body is "Dead," and subsequent stanzas indicate a purely spiritual existence:

For *Sight* inherits Beauty, *Hearing* Sounds,
 The *Nostril* Sweet Perfumes,
 All *Tastes* have hidden Rooms
Within the *Tongue*; and *Feeling Feeling* Wounds
 With Pleasure and Delight: but I
 Forgot the rest, and was all Sight, or Ey.
 Unbodied and Devoid of Care,
Just as in Heavn the Holy Angels are. (33-38)

Since he describes himself as "unbodied," his "Body being Dead," and distinguishes himself from all senses but sight, we are apt to read "newly clothd with skin" metaphorically. Although he is merely concerned to express how and what he felt and perceived, Traherne nonetheless creates the impression of one who remembers not only pre-linguistic or pre-natal existence, put *pre-incarnate* existence as well.

This adumbration is by no means consistent throughout Traherne's writings, however. At the beginning of the *Centuries*, for example, he writes that "an empty book is like an Infant's Soul, in which anything may be written. It is capable of all things, but containeth nothing" (3). We should remember, however, that his main concern in this passage is to describe the empty book he has begun to write in, not to describe the actual state of an infant's soul. Furthermore, he speaks here of a generic infant in what sounds to me like a formulaic expression, whereas his poems speak of personal memories. In the poems, we find more equivocal statements such as that in "The Salutation":

> When silent I,
> So many thousand thousand yeers,
> Beneath the Dust did in a Chaos lie,
> How could I Smiles or Tears,
> Or Lips or Hands or Eys or Ears perceiv?
> Welcom ye Treasures which I now receiv. (7-12)

Traherne clearly postulates some point when he did not exist, but this does not preclude his belief in the kind of pre-incarnate existence implied in "The Preparative."

One might ascribe Traherne's reluctance to speak more positively of pre-existence to the fact that he was an Anglican divine and found the notion far too shadowy to recommend to faith. On the other hand, he was writing at a time when the Cambridge Neoplatonists—writers like Ralph Cudworth, Thomas Burnet, and Henry More, respectable Anglicans themselves—were writing on the pre-existence of the soul as though it were part of Christian revelation, and Plato a patriarch. As George Meyer points out, Wordsworth was familiar with some of these Neoplatonists as well (Meyer 36). Why, then, would Wordsworth and Traherne be reluctant to invoke these precedents and speak openly about pre-existence, if they really entertained such a belief?

As I have argued, pre-existence in Wordsworth is intimately bound up with his recollections of "infant sensibility," just as Traherne's descriptions of "unbodied" existence are part of his alleged "pure and virgin apprehensions"; here, I think, is where the anxiety about heresy might come into play. As Franz Wöhrer explains, to assert that an infant comes into the world *without sin* is to deny the necessity, and therefore possibly even the efficacy, of infant baptism:

> Traherne's views on the beginning of the child's mystical awareness are in many ways original, but contradict the orthodox theology of Original Sin. In the orthodox doctrine God's Presence in the soul of man becomes possible only after the purification of the soul through baptism. (99)

In a milieu where the Church of England was asserting a monolithic privilege over various dissenting groups, Traherne must have recognized the potential infelicity of revealing his personal convictions on the subject of childhood. It seems to have been quite acceptable for Anglicans to believe in pre-existence; but for one to posit an unfallen state among infants would be to play into the hands of the Anabaptists, for example, who advocated adult baptism. This concern for orthodoxy seems a likely reason for Traherne's not publishing his poems, and for his brother Philip's not publishing them even after preparing them for the printer. Whether it was also the reason for Thomas's reluctance to embrace pre-existence must remain uncertain; but I would sooner attribute this reluctance to a proclivity to record only his recollections and feelings, without drawing any conclusions from these.

From the point of view of modern scientific orthodoxy, Traherne is guilty of far graver heresies, of course. Although I have been countenancing his claims, one ought obviously to regard them with some degree of scepticism. Many readers are likely to reject outright any claim to pre- and perinatal recollections, as Traherne scholars of the past have done:

> There are critics who categorically dismiss Traherne's claim as self-delusion or romantic speculation on the part of the poet. Other critics reject it...from a scientific point of view, as entirely untenable. The majority of scholars read Traherne's "mystic child" in terms of a conventional literary metaphor with symbolic import, originating in the Gospel, rather than as a poetic transcription of experience. (Wöhrer 149)

As Wöhrer goes on to point out, however, one of the problems presented by such symbolic readings of Traherne is that the poet is quite emphatic in rejecting "curling Metaphors" and "painted eloquence" ("The Author to the Critical Peruser" lines 11-12). These rejections might be a mere pose, but the hermeneutic circuity Wöhrer requires to extract a convincing symbolic reading from the poems suggests the candour of Traherne's artless intentions (Wöhrer 160-161). Nor is Traherne's the only recorded testimony of awareness in the womb: the fifteenth-century Swiss saint, Niklaus von Flüe, claimed to have seen "a star in the heavens that lit up the whole world" even "before he was born" (Yates 40). It remains, however, what Wöhrer formulates as the "pivotal question," "whether the embryonic cerebrum in the ninth uterine month is capable of awareness at all" (162)—assuming that memory is confined to the cerebrum. This is an issue germane to our reading of Wordsworth as well, for if his "shadowy recollections" stem from life in the womb as Traherne describes it, we may be able to reduce both of their intimations of consciousness in God to consciousness in the womb.

Science, Pre-natal Consciousness, and Pre-existence

In his discussion of the issue in his study of Traherne, Wöhrer cites several scientific authorities who support the possibility of pre-natal consciousness. He credits William Walter with the discovery of late-term cerebral activities through EEG recordings,[8] a finding supported by later researchers (Wöhrer 162-63). With reservations, Wöhrer also introduces the inferences of psychoanalyst G. H. Graber, who contends that "the unborn child enjoys a state of 'rapturous well-being'... and that it has an intense awareness of 'one-ness'" (163-64). This state is inferred by Graber and other psychoanalysts from the "retrogressive urge" of adults who seek the experience of oneness (Wöhrer 164).

The *kind* of consciousness Walter's EEG recordings discover is not, of course, accessible; we might be able to tell if the fetus is asleep or awake, but we cannot tell if it is remembering or reasoning. Evidence from hypnotherapy, however, provides clues to the kind of awareness infants may possess at delivery and in the womb. A number of recent articles in the *Pre- and Perinatal Psychology Journal* present case studies of persons hypnotically regressed to birth and pre-birth for therapeutic purposes, regressions which elicited detailed memories that are in some instances corroborated by parents. The majority of these articles are by David Cheek, an obstetrician, gynaecologist, and hypnotherapist; and by David Chamberlain, President (1995) of the Association for Pre- and Perinatal Psychology and Health. Since these case studies can at this point convince us only through therapy transcripts, I ask the reader's indulgence as I cite some of these at length.

Cheek discusses several cases of what he calls "telepathic fetal awareness," a term suggested to him by his subjects' reports of details in their environments before their birth, reports later corroborated by their mothers. For example, "Dee," a patient Cheek was treating for depression, crippling back pain, and recurrent dreams that her mother was trying to abort her with a button hook, produced a frightening womb memory under hypnosis that suggested knowledge of her mother's intent to abort her:

A: Appearing very agitated and breathing rapidly, she said, It's before I'm born. My father is shouting, "I'm going to kill you." (A few seconds later, Dee began screaming. She pulled her legs up to her chest as though trying to get away from something very frightening…. She became more relaxed again and was able to talk.) "I saw that button hook coming up at me. I knew my mother was trying to get me out."

Q: Then what happened?

A: Nothing happened—only a little bleeding. (130)

Cheek reports that he received a handwritten note from his subject's mother confirming her husband's threats and the abortion attempt (which occurred at about the sixth month of pregnancy) and attesting to what we would assume in such a case, namely that the child "had no way of knowing about these incidents" (130). Barring the client's or therapist's wholesale fabrication of the account,[9] we must conclude that Cheek's client subconsciously remembered the events before her birth or, less likely, accurately "guessed" what had occurred.

Another client wanted insight into the circumstances that prompted the obstetrician at his birth to use forceps in the delivery, an emergency procedure that had left a deep physical scar. Through hypnotic regression, the client first arrives at a point shortly before his mother went into labour, and he describes a scene at which his mother has just learned of his grandfather's death, a scene with details later verified by his mother (Cheek 133). This leads to a description of the onset of labour and birth:

Q: Where are you?

A: Inside. (Now, he begins moving his head from side to side, moving his arms and legs in an alternating, coordinated way….)

Q: What is happening now?

A: My mother is in labor. (The movements continue. He is partially reliving the scene but at the same time is able to comment as though he is a bystander. His walking and head movements continued during a silent twenty seconds.)

Q: What is happening now?

A: My mother is afraid of dying, like her father. They were very close. Her labor stops. I'm stuck and they are trying to put forceps on my head. My head is trying to get away from the forceps. (132)

Cheek comments that his client's description accords with obstetric facts which the man "did not consciously know" but which could be experienced from the point of view of the baby:

[U]terine contractions will stop being expulsive and the cervix will stop dilating when a mother is in great pain or is frightened. Apparently her fear had activated the same feeling in him. The effect of her epinephrine [an adrenaline hormone], or more likely his own epinephrine, would have accelerated his metabolism and increased his need for oxygen. The slowing of his heart rate after a contraction would reflect oxygen deprivation to his brain and would have alarmed the obstetrician and prompted him to try immediate delivery of the baby. (132-33)

Based on this and other cases, Cheek concludes that the embryo or fetus "is a feeling and interpreting organism" which mirrors its mother's feelings about her environment, and which receives "telepathic and/or clairvoyant" information from her. These speculations would accord with the memories of Traherne and Wordsworth as well; if pre- and perinatal memories can be accessed in a hypnotic state, it is conceivable that certain persons may be able to remember them consciously.

Womb memories, according to David Chamberlain, "are nearly as common as birth memories" in hypnotherapy. He cites a number of such cases from both his and other therapists' findings,[10] and concludes that infants come into the world "already thinking persons." The same hypnotherapy research that introduces memory into pre-natal life takes it even further, however. Chamberlain gives examples from among his own clients who claim to recall circumstances around the time of their *conception*. Although it is not clear whether the accounts were corroborated by the respective parents (or whether this was possible), it seems to me that the sheer bathos of the material recommends its authenticity; we are not given wishful visions of parental harmony, and we must wonder what the motive behind these accounts is if they are not in some sense experiential:

> For example, Ingrid remembered her mother and father making love on a couch in Germany, before they were married. The doorbell rang to announce that Grandmother and Aunt had come back from shopping when they weren't supposed to. The encounter sent shockwaves through all present.... Another client, Ida, remembered trouble at her conception: "It wasn't right then," she said. "Mother was not in the condition for me to come in. She was drunk. It didn't seem right.... She was mad at dad, forced to be there. She didn't want me there; it was just an accident. I could see that the time wasn't right for me to come in; I knew." (181-82)

As I expect any curious person would, Chamberlain asks his client *where she is* if she is not "in":

> Ida said she did not take up residence in her mother for three weeks and spent the interim floating in a comfortable place hard to describe and hard to leave. There were special swirls of light that felt good. "It's real peaceful," she said. "I wish I could share it with you. It makes me want to cry because it feels so good." (182)

The similarity of this apparently pre-incarnate memory to the experience expressed in Traherne's "The Preparative" is remarkable: his "*vital Sun* that round about did *ray*" in a state "Unbodied and Devoid of Care" sounds very much like the therapy subject's "comfortable place" with its "swirls of light" ("The Preparative" 18; 37). Equally striking is the parallel in Wordsworth's Ode, where "not in utter nakedness / But trailing clouds of glory do we come / From God, who is our home" (63-65). Wordsworth apparently assumes that the "comfortable place" is Abraham's bosom, God.

Chamberlain is quick to point out the incommensurability of his findings with received notions about the supposed basis of memory and consciousness in neurophysiology; and the same notions may still prevent us from taking Wordsworth, Vaughan, Traherne, and Chamberlain's subjects seriously. On the other hand, some renowned neuroscientists do not accept the hypothesis that memory must be entirely confined to the brain; Wilder Penfield and John C. Eccles have written in favour of a dualist theory of mind-brain that would facilitate immaterial memories in addition to immaterial psyches.

Eccles, who has published many books on the mind-brain issue,[11] is more recent (1994) in supporting a dualist position "that the mind and brain are independent entities" (*How the Self Controls its Brain* 9). He defends this view on the grounds that it can account for the fact that "multifarious neural events in our cerebral cortex can from moment to moment give us global mental experiences with a unitary character," something which has always "been beyond explanation by any mind-brain theory" (*How the Self* 179). Eccles (with Friedrich Beck) also addresses a typical objection to the dualist position, namely that it implies the input of an unknown mental energy to effect neural response, an input which would violate the law of conservation of energy in physics:

> Because of the conservation laws of physics, it has been generally
> believed that non-material mental events can have no effective
> action on neuronal events in the brain. On the contrary, it has
> been proposed that all mental experiences have a unitary composi-
> tion, the units being unique for each type of experience and called
> *psychons*. It has been further hypothesized that each psychon is
> linked in a unitary manner to a specific dendron, which is the
> basis of mind-brain interaction. (*How the Self* 141)

Mental events, according to this hypothesis, influence material events
"in a manner analogous to the probability fields of quantum mechanics,"
fields which "carry neither mass nor energy, but which nevertheless can
exert effective action at microsites" *(How the Self* 71; 56). What is important about Eccles's difficult explanation is that it requires an *immaterial*
entity ("the psychon complex of the self") that "must be endowed also
with 'memories' that are continuously up-dated for efficient action"; the
immaterial self "must have the memory to act with speed and skill in calling into action the appropriate stored memories in the brain" (*How the
Self* 179). Eccles's theory finally leads him "to attribute the uniqueness of
the self or soul to a supernatural spiritual creation," and he suggests that
"[m]aterialist explanation of the mind-brain problem... can now be recognized as unscientific and even as superstitions that have lingered too
long" (*How the Self* 180; 168).

A similarly dualistic conclusion is reached by Wilder Penfield who, as a
neurosurgeon at the Montreal Neurological Institute, pioneered the evo-
cation of memories through electrical stimulation of the brain. Penfield
considers the mind to be essentially separate from the brain (54), and
although he holds that the mind depends on the brain for its memory
storage, he speculates about the possibility of an additional, immaterial
memory:

If the mind had any separate awareness while the highest brain-mechanism is inactive, it could make some use of a memory mechanism of its own. But the engram for mind-memory would have to be redefined. Instead of being the "lasting trace" left in an organism by "psychic experience," it would be the lasting trace left on psychic structure by neuronal action! (50)

In Penfield's view, as in Eccles's, immaterial mental structures remain dependent upon material structures, so the kinds of pre-incarnate memories alleged by Chamberlain's subject and intimated by the poets are still inexplicable in neurophysiological terms; however, one could conceivably reconcile these memories to the views of Penfield and Eccles, since their hypotheses at least allow for the possibility of superphysical consciousness, whereas this is ruled out in materialist paradigms.

Chamberlain reconciles the facts of neuroscience with his own discoveries through Rupert Sheldrake's hypothesis of morphogenetic fields (Chamberlain 182). According to this hypothesis, morphogenetic, or morphic, fields organize the characteristic structure of all "morphic units"—atoms, crystals, organisms, patterns of instinctive behaviour, memories, etc.[12] Applying his notion to memory, Sheldrake posits that the reason no one has ever found a recognizable memory trace in the material patterns of the brain is that

> memories are *not* stored in the brain. The spatio-temporal patterns we remember may not be inscribed in the brain in the form of material traces but may depend instead on morphic fields. The morphic fields through which our experience, behaviour, and mental activity were organized in the past can become present again by morphic resonance. We remember because of this resonance from ourselves in the past. (197)

In this paradigm, brain damage results in memory loss not because the memories themselves have been damaged, but because the morphic field they constitute "cannot be tuned in" through an appropriate pattern of brain activity (218-19). This interpretation of memory loss

> makes it much easier to understand the fact that lost abilities often return; patients often recover partially or completely from brain damage even though the damaged regions of the brain do not regenerate. The appropriate patterns of activity come into operation somewhere else in the brain. This is almost impossible to understand if programs are "hard-wired" into the nervous system; but fields can move their regions of activity and reorganize themselves in a way that fixed material structures cannot. (219)

Since Sheldrake's hypothesis posits an immaterial basis in fields for both organized consciousness and memory, this would seem to imply the possibility of consciousness (as conceived by Eccles) within a morphic field not presently associated with a physical body. It would follow that the memory of such a state would be very difficult to access, since its "form," its morphic field, would be thoroughly alien to a consciousness habituated to a physical body; one would have to shut out the interference of this habituation in order to access pre-incarnate memory, as is perhaps facilitated by hypnosis, near-death experiences, and perhaps even *imagination*, as some of the Romantics conceived of and cultivated it. The extent to which writers like Traherne and Wordsworth were able to attain to such a disembodied consciousness in their adult lives would therefore determine the success with which they were able to recall prenatal experience, or even those memories of the infant consciousness so alien to us. If this explanation remains uncomfortably foreign to the reader's basic beliefs about the world, I believe it is nonetheless the simplest, most practical way of elucidating and synthesizing the testimony of the poets. They are simply writing down what they remember to be true.

As I hope to have demonstrated, the explanatory value of contemporary hypnotherapy accounts and modern theories of memory are such that these ought to be incorporated into an interpretation of Wordsworth, Traherne, and Vaughan. If scholarly research in the humanities can continue to countenance the speculations of Freud, Jung, and Lacan—speculations far less convincing, in my view—we ought to be able to employ the findings of more recent researchers into the nature of consciousness, insofar as these are applicable to certain authors. In Wordsworth's case, this approach promises to yield not only an explanation of his more obscure passages, but may also offer us a means to *enjoying* his work, and especially the Immortality Ode, even more: if we, too, can believe in a kind of pre-existence, we benefit from the added pleasure of seeing our shadowy notions expressed so brilliantly. We can also be certain that Wordsworth, at least, was not inventing a memory of pre-existence to impress his friends or to sell books, since his memory could do little more than alienate him from most of his audience at that time.

Pre-existence, Supersensible Perception, and the Spiritual Science of Rudolf Steiner

As Joseph Head and S. L. Cranston's encyclopaedic *Reincarnation in World Thought* illustrates, and as Wordsworth points out in the Fenwick note, the notion of a pre-existent state is not confined to Plato and has "entered into the popular creeds of many nations" (*PW* 4.464). It is, in fact, indigenous to the cultures of many aboriginal peoples on every continent of the earth, though generally as part of a belief in re-incarnation.[13] One might draw a number of parallels between these traditions and the notion as it appears in Wordsworth, but many of these traditions are expressed in vague terms and therefore unsuited to my clarificatory aims. The discussion of pre-existence in the work of Rudolf Steiner (1861-1925), on the other hand, is in the form of scientific investigation and comes with many insights into the nature of mysticism and supersensible perception, which he distinguishes. In particular, Steiner's remarks on the gradual loss of a sense for the spiritual in nature *over the course of human evolution* will provide us with yet another parallel for Wordsworth's personal loss, and will finally connect this loss to the intimation of a pre-existent state.

The corpus of Steiner's work is so extensive, and yet so foreign to the mainstream of modern thought, that some explanation of his methods and findings will be necessary for these to bear any credit or intelligibility.[14] Many of the things he says regarding "the life between death and rebirth," as he formulates it, might be found in the *Upanishads*, Proclus's *Platonic Theology*, or Madame Blavatsky's *Isis Unveiled*; but a great deal is unique in Steiner. Furthermore, his work is presented in a form commensurate with the twentieth-century philosopher and Goethe scholar he was.[15] Steiner's research, however much he communicated it using terms from ancient traditions, is always presented as *his* observations of the supersensible, and always expressed in as naturalistic a manner as possible. His claim to greater perspicacity in these observations compared with other seers—Jakob Böhme, Emmanuel Swedenborg, or Annie Besant, for example—was that he saw with much fuller consciousness and applied to his observations the principles of modern science.[16] This area of investigation he termed "spiritual science" (*Geistesforschung*), or alternatively, *anthroposophy*.

Put simply, what Steiner claims to be able to do is to see into a supersensible or spiritual world in which a variety of phenomena are observable, and which is intimately connected to the sensible world. This ability is something he claims is dormant in everyone and can be cultivated through certain exercises (*Esoteric Development passim*); to use a crude analogy, organs for supersensible perception may be developed just as a microscope may be developed to see *subsensible* worlds. A number of things recommend Steiner's claim: first, he does not advance anything that is not conceivably reconcilable with natural scientific *facts*, although he contradicts many *theories*; second, his descriptions of supersensible worlds present a consistency over hundreds of lectures and many books, such as we should expect from any scientific body of knowledge; third, and most importantly, his statements about the effects of supersensible agencies within the sensible world have led to proven, practical applications in pedagogy, medicine, agriculture, and even mechanics.[17] The precedent of these practical applications is, I think, sufficient to allow me to introduce Steiner's statements as creditable observations that will have a practical application in elucidating the psychology of supersensible perception and beliefs in pre-existence.

The relationship of Steiner's experiences to those of the mystics is discussed in his *Autobiography*:

> If a mystic sets out to describe the world of spirit, one is justified in telling him: You are speaking of your personal experience; what you describe is subjective. It was not my spiritual task to follow a mystical path to the spirit.
>
> It was my task to create a basis for Anthroposophy through a thinking as objective as scientific thinking that does not stop short at merely registering the sense-perceptible facts, but advances to comprehensive knowledge.... Through this objective cognition, free of mystical feeling, I transmitted my experience of the spiritual world. (358)

Elsewhere, Steiner claims that what many other clairvoyants possess is an atavism from a time when people "entered the spiritual world in a more instinctive, unconscious way" (*Evolution of Consciousness* 80), unlike his "objective" approach to the supersensible. The obvious analogy here is the difference between random, emotionally-laden observations of the sense world and the attempts at objective observation in Baconian science. This is not merely a distinction made by Steiner, for anyone can discern differences between his expositions and the writings of the mystics. Nowhere in his work does he speak in terms of experiencing the "oneness" of the universe as the *end* of his investigation; although he says that those who meditate with the object of "dissolving... in the Universal All" are led to "spiritual percep-tions," such persons are "without full consciousness" of these perceptions and are "not able to distinguish whether the things they experience spring from egotism or not" (*Esoteric Development* 173). He acknowledges a super-sensible unity, but he is at pains to describe the diversity of the higher worlds.[18]

Part of this diversity lies in what Steiner calls the "Akashic Record" (a term employed by H. P. Blavatsky as well), a kind of permanent reflection of spiritual history:

> [F]or spiritual research the facts even of the remote past have not disappeared.... They leave their impressions, their exact counter-parts, behind in the spiritual foundations of the world, and he who, penetrating the visible world, is able to lift his perception into the invisible, is finally able to have before him something that might be compared with a mighty spiritual panorama, in which all past world-processes are recorded. These imperishable impressions of all that is spiritual may be called the "Akashic Record".... (105)

By combining his "reading" of this record with known historical facts, Steiner presents us with a history of consciousness that, as we might expect, traverses the boundaries of birth and death. (Since a great deal of this material comes to us as transcribed lectures, it is not always clear whether Steiner speaks from supersensible observation or traditional his-torical research.) If one is not willing to accept this history as science, one ought at least to accept it as an imaginative reconstruction of the past, the half part of which, I am certain, could not be reduced to a mere combina-tion of historical, theosophical, and literary tradition.[19]

Typical of Steiner's historical perception/ reconstructions are his state-ments about the awareness of pre-existence in ancient peoples:

A few thousand years ago, even the most primitive man would never have questioned the presence in his soul of something brought down with him from the supersensible into the life of the senses; it was an everyday experience in his dreamlike imaginations. (*Evolution of Consciousness* 39)

What is significant about this for our study of Wordsworth is the relationship to the external world that attends these ancient intimations:

A man in those days had a feeling of intense sadness when looking at all that was most lovely in the sense-world. He looked at the flowers, springing out of the Earth in their wonderful beauty, and watched the blossoms unfold.... He saw the loveliness of the springs bubbling forth in shady places, and his senses spoke to him of their refreshing powers. But then... he said to himself: "It seems as though all this has fallen—fallen through sin from the world I bear within me and which I have brought down into physical existence out of spiritual worlds." (*EC* 39-40)

We find in this characterization a striking parallel to Wordsworth's complaint in the Immortality Ode, that "there hath past away a glory from the earth" even though "lovely is the rose" and "Waters on a starry night / Are beautiful and fair" (11-18). Based on Steiner's assertions, it would appear that Wordsworth has retained the consciousness not only of an earlier period in his ontogenetic development, but also in the phylogenetic development of humankind.

According to Steiner, the remedy for the ancients' sadness lay in the teachings of the Mysteries, teachings which are largely unrecorded since the students of these schools were sworn to secrecy.[20] It was the task of these schools "to point out how the divine-spiritual dwells in all things, even in those of the senses. It was the spirituality of nature that these teachers had to make clear" (*EC* 40). In other words, the despairing ancient was told that "what is living in you lives also outside in nature" (40). Hence, we might see Wordsworth's consolation, his memories of a "primal sympathy" with nature (Ode 182), as a replication of these Mystery teachings. In addition to this consolation, Wordsworth benefits from the intimation of pre-existence which, according to Steiner, is precisely what people today need to be reminded of.

As for the reason behind the child's willingness to "provoke" the loss of his connection to the spiritual—what Wordsworth is unable to answer in the eighth stanza of the Ode—the answer to this is forthcoming in Steiner as well, although it may be disappointingly simple. Bound up with the instinctive clairvoyance of the ancients there was, he says, a kind of determinism: a deterministic guidance from spiritual sources that had to be overcome through disconnection from the supersensible:

> Hence we can say that, looked at from the spiritual world, people have lost a great deal precisely because in the course of their evolution they have had to be led towards freedom.... And now [1923] is the historical point of time when a striving to regain what has been lost must begin. (*EC* 79-80)

Insofar as a child's development is a recapitulation of human evolution, and insofar as an instinctive clairvoyance lingers in a child as it seems to have done in Wordsworth and Traherne, the child's development necessitates the same kind of loss Steiner observes in the species. The "best Philosopher" puts by the "Presence which is not to be put by" (Ode 121) in order to achieve freedom—freedom, with all the potential for error and vice it brings, as Traherne observed.

That Wordsworth possessed a supersensible faculty comparable to one of three discussed by Steiner may be inferred from the relationship between the imagination and the faculty in question as this relationship is implied by both authors. In chapter 2, I concluded that for Wordsworth, the cultivation of the imaginative faculty is necessary to create an opening in consciousness into which "visitations" of the "presence" may enter (see page 24). A similar process is indicated by Steiner when he writes of how "a spiritual content is *directly perceived* and lights up within the imagination" (*Autobiography* 382). When Steiner describes the first of three levels of supersensible perception, he terms it *Imagination,* or imaginative cognition, but makes it clear he means something distinct from common imagination (the other levels are Inspiration and Intuition, which he defines equally idiosyncratically). The "Imaginations" perceived through this faculty "are the first supersensible impressions that we can have" (*Esoteric Development* 88). Similarly, Wordsworth attempts to expand the meaning of imagination to suit his experience: as Grob notes, the poet affirms "a suprasensuous reality whose contents can be read by a special human faculty correspondingly liberated from sense that Wordsworth uneasily terms 'Imagination'" (Grob 239). That Wordsworth and Steiner may be talking about the same thing is suggested by Steiner's assertion that in the first level of supersensible perception (Imagination) we see "back to our birth," whereas through Inspiration "we look beyond conception and birth... and behold ourselves as we were before we came down from spiritual worlds."[21] If Wordsworth could remember "from the dawn almost / Of life," he must have possessed *Imagination* in the sense of a supersensible faculty.

Steiner describes the conditions of consciousness obtaining not only in the youth of civilization, but in his own youth as well: and he, too, "would have felt the sense-world as spiritual darkness" had it "not received light from that other world" (*Autobiography* 30). Many of his experiences seem to parallel Wordsworth, only in Steiner's case they appear much more pronounced and are described with a singular perspicacity:

> I was then at an age [30-33] when by inclination one turns intensively toward one's surroundings, seeking to establish a firm connection with external life.... And I began to realize how very difficult it had been for me during childhood and youth to relate

myself to the outer world through the senses. I had always found it difficult to commit to memory external data that has to be assimilated, for example in the study of science. I had to observe natural objects repeatedly in order to be able to identify them and to know their scientific classification. The external world really appeared to me somewhat shadow-like or picture-like. It moved past me like pictures, whereas my relationship with the spiritual always had the character of concrete reality. (*Autobiography* 205-06)

It seems to me that what Steiner describes here is a more pronounced version of the "abyss of idealism" that Wordsworth mentions in the Fenwick note, a state of mind which makes the sensible world appear somehow less substantial. It should be clear, however, that "abyss of idealism" is an inappropriate formulation insofar as it suggests complete absorption in mere ideas. What Steiner experiences is the "concrete reality" of a spiritual world. Wordsworth probably expressed himself better when he described his feelings in childhood as "my absolute spirituality" (*Memoirs* 2.486).

Judging by the parallels I have adduced, I think it justifiable to conclude that Wordsworth's experience may be clarified to some degree through "Spiritual Science," a conclusion that will receive further support from parallels drawn in the next chapter. Even if the reader should discover a way of reducing the claims of both Wordsworth and Steiner to more conventional, materialistic explanations, one ought to recognize the value of discovering in these disparate claims a consistency and interrelation that might aid even such a reductive project. On the other hand, one should also consider the possibility that the supersensible world these men saw with their Imagination is as real as the sensible one with which we are familiar.

Chapter 4

New Light on the Ode

In the foregoing chapters, I have already commented on a number of passages from Wordsworth's Immortality Ode, working from the informing ideas of pre-existence and supersensible perception back into the poem. At this point, I wish to examine in detail several contentious passages from the poem and apply to these a reading synthesized from my exploration of those informing ideas, as well as from the context of the other authors I have introduced. Although I will engage earlier critical commentary on these passages, the bulk of this engagement I defer to subsequent chapters.

The "Tree, of many, one"

Several of the lines in the third and fourth stanzas of the Immortality Ode are a source of perennial mystification because of their vague allusiveness. The "timely utterance" of line 23, which Trilling suggests might be the poem "Resolution and Independence" (Trilling 139), could refer to just about anything; the "fields of sleep" in line 28 seem to allude to something mythological but recede like a dream from explicatory gropings; and the capitalized Tree, Field, and Pansy of the fourth stanza tantalizingly invite symbolic associations. I do not pretend to discover Rosicrucian mysteries in these, but I think there is good evidence that the "Tree, of many, one" (line 51) is—and this may disappoint somewhat—a favourite ash tree of the poet's at Cambridge. De Selincourt suggests this identification as well (*PW* 4.466) but does not point out its particular significance: as Wordsworth tells us in *The Prelude*, the ash tree was often the site of his "tranquil visions" of "bright appearances," visions that would correspond to the "something that is gone" of the Ode.

Other significations have, of course, been suggested for the Tree. The Tree of Knowledge is a possible referent, especially if one reads the poem bearing in mind Wordsworth's statement, that the fall of Man presents an analogy in favour of pre-existence (*PW* 4.464). Marjorie Levinson seizes upon the possibility that Wordsworth alludes to the Tree of Liberty; "Wordsworth was of course, familiar with this commonplace symbol" of the French Revolution (109). Since the Tree (along with the Field, which Levinson facilely equates with the Champ de Mars) reminds Wordsworth "of something that is gone," it accords quite well with such an identification; Wordsworth had, of course, long since lost faith in the "glory" of the Revolution. Unfortunately, such a reading must disregard much of the Ode, as well as the entirety of the Fenwick note and Wordsworth's earlier remarks on his poem. For example, in a letter to Catherine Clarkson of 1814, he writes that "the poem rests entirely upon two recollections of childhood, one that of a splendour in the objects of sense which is passed away, and the other an indisposition to bend to the law of death as applying to our particular case."[1] Following through with Levinson's argument, we would call Wordsworth's indications here a misreading of his own poem: we must suppose he is repressing the real meaning, perhaps trying to "liberate the fond, pastoral memory from its original, political context" (Levinson 110). I think we ought to apply the little-regarded axiom of

Occam to such readings, namely that suppositions should not be multiplied unnecessarily when simple explanations are available.

De Selincourt provides several other options for interpretation in his notes to the Ode. He suggests the "tall ash" described in Book Fourth of *The Prelude* (86-92) and the "single tree" of Book Sixth. This "single tree," one of Wordsworth's haunts at Cambridge, was clearly very significant to the poet:

> A single tree
> There was, no doubt yet standing there, an ash,
> With sinuous trunk, boughs exquisitely wreathed:
>
>   *   *   *   *
>
> Oft have I stood
> Foot-bound uplooking at this lovely tree
> Beneath a frosty moon. The hemisphere
> Of magic fiction, verse of mine perhaps
> May never tread, but scarcely Spenser's self
> Could have more tranquil visions in his youth,
> More bright appearances could scarcely see
> Of human forms and superhuman powers,
> Than I beheld standing on winter nights
> Alone beneath this fairy work of earth. (6.90-109)

Not only is this a "single tree"—"of many, one"—it is described as the site of those "visitations" from the supersensible that Wordsworth still enjoyed in his youth. I think there can be little question that the "bright appearances" and "tranquil visions" of this passage correspond to the "something that is gone" that the Tree speaks of in the Ode (53), as well as to the "vision splendid" of stanza 5. I therefore dispute not only Levinson's claims about political allegory, but also those readings of the Ode which try to see the first four stanzas as somehow disconnected from the visionary themes that cannot be avoided from stanza 5 forward.[2] By discovering in the Tree an allusion (regrettably private) to a time and place where the "Presence" still made itself felt, we may claim here another manifestation of the consistent theme of lost supersensible perceptions in the early stanzas of the Ode.

"Behold the Child": Hartley Coleridge?

Since I have presented a great deal of material linking the autobiographical *Prelude* to the Immortality Ode, a reading that posits Hartley Coleridge as the child in stanza 7 must appear incommensurate with my approach. The extended, 1815 title—"Ode: Intimations of Immortality from Recollections of Early Childhood"—is perfectly appropriate when we accept that Wordsworth's introduction of the incarnation account (stanzas 5-8) is based on self-observation, not observations of other children. On the other hand, the poet seems to think he can universalize these self-observations; as Curtis points out, Wordsworth often assumes that "his own feelings are pertinent and meaningful to all men" (147). Insofar as Wordsworth projected his assumptions onto Hartley, I think it is still possible that Hartley was the inspiration for parts of the Ode. Of course, this is an idea advanced regularly by critics since John Rea in 1928,[3] but I wish to suggest that Hartley might have reminded Wordsworth of his own past, not that he provided the poet with a model for childhood in general.

Wordsworth appears to recognize some idiosyncrasy in his prolonged access to what I have identified as perinatal consciousness; in *The Prelude*, he writes of how the "infant sensibility…was *in me* / Augmented and sustained" (2.285-87; emphasis mine). Although he no doubt suspected that such was not the case with everyone, there was good reason to suspect it of Hartley, whose curious behaviour may have led Wordsworth to think that his experience was more prevalent than it actually was and is. Thomas McFarland notes a passage from Crabb Robinson's diary that would, to a believer in pre-existence, suggest Hartley's incomplete naturalization to his physical body:

> Hartley, when about five, was asked a question by someone concerning himself calling him "Hartley." "Which Hartley?" asked the boy. "Why, is there more than one Hartley?" "Yes," he replied, "there is a deal of Hartleys." "How so?" "There's Picture Hartley" (Hazlitt had painted a portrait of him) "and Shadow Hartley, and there's Echo Hartley, and there's Catch-me-fast Hartley," at the same time seizing his own arm with the other hand very eagerly.... [4]

McFarland goes on to assume, I think correctly, that Coleridge had circulated this story long before Crabb Robinson wrote it down in 1811. One might even suppose that Wordsworth was present when Hartley said these things. If he was, he could only have been impressed by "'Catch-me-fast Hartley'...seizing his own arm," just as Wordsworth recalled having as a child seized "something that resisted, to be sure that there was anything outside me."[5] The decentred ego implied by Hartley's proliferation of identities might have led Wordsworth to think that the boy had not incarnated fully yet, and part of him still resided in "Abraham's bosom."[6]

Even more striking is Crabb Robinson's characterization of young Hartley as living in an abyss of idealism:

> Hartley when a boy had no pleasure in things; they made no impression on him, till they had undergone a certain process in his mind and were become thoughts or feelings. (1.44)

The behaviour that Crabb Robinson observes here may well have reminded Wordsworth of his own childhood, when he "was sure of [his] own mind" but felt that "everything else fell away, and vanished into thought" (*PW* 4.467).

Based on this evidence, I think we could claim that Hartley was some kind of catalyst to the Ode, but only insofar as he reminded the poet of his former self. To state positively, with Lucy Newlyn, that "the child of the *Intimations is* Hartley Coleridge" is going too far; the child is at best a composite of Hartley and Wordsworth. We cannot ignore the biographical implications of the full title of 1815, "Ode: Intimations of Immortality from Recollections of Early Childhood." Furthermore, we cannot ignore the evidence from the variations of the Ode discovered by Jared Curtis and published already in 1970. In the poet's apostrophe to the "best Philosopher," whom Newlyn takes for Hartley, Wordsworth toyed with some lines that reveal the biographical basis of the address:

> I speak not in delusion—but from feeling
> Of my past self, an insight, a revealing
> And trusting to the same
> Child as Thou art I give thee highest name,
> Thou best Philosopher.... (Curtis 142)

Curtis concludes that Wordsworth "wants it clear that he refers not to Hartley Coleridge,... as most commentators point out, nor to children in general, as Coleridge assumed, but to himself" (145). As we ought, perhaps, to expect, this is a conclusion in perfect accord with the elaborate title Wordsworth appends to the Ode in 1815, in which we are plainly told that it is based on his recollections of early childhood.

The Soul's Immensity

It seems to me peculiar that Wordsworth speaks of the *size* of the soul in line 110 of the Ode. Despite the possibility of abstracting the "Soul's immensity" to mean "greatness of soul," I find the word *immensity* an intractably spatial substantive. Since the soul in Christian tradition is generally conceived of as being the same size as the physical body,[7] I think we should ascribe Wordsworth's idiosyncratic characterization to his recollections rather than to religious tradition. As we can furthermore gather by the alleged observations of Steiner and the self-observation of Traherne, this feeling of having had extension beyond the limits of the physical body is related to supersensible perceptions and pre-existence.

We can easily connect the "Soul's immensity" to Wordsworth's statements in the Fenwick note, in which he recalls his feeling that everything he looked upon seemed "inherent in" his "immaterial nature" in childhood; if he felt the world to be in his soul, he might reasonably describe his soul as "immense." In an effort to clarify this experience, Trilling draws upon Freud's theory of the individuation of the ego:

> Originally the ego includes everything, later it detaches from itself the outside world. The ego-feeling we are aware of now is thus only a shrunken vestige of a more extensive feeling—a feeling which embraced the universe and expressed an inseparable connection of the ego with the external world. (Freud, *Civilization and its Discontents*; qtd. in Trilling 144)

Freud, who must speculate because he cannot see the ego nor feel the "more extensive feeling," attests to that which Wordsworth claims actually to remember. But for all its metaphysical suggestiveness, Freud's account remains reconciled with materialist assumptions; there is only a *feeling* of greater extension, a feeling that must be delusive since the physical brain that supposedly houses the ego remains a constant size. Although we might explain the watered-down testimony of the Fenwick note through Freud, the asserted *reality* of the Ode-child's "Soul's immensity" is better explained through spiritual psychology. A more pertinent and elucidating passage appears in Steiner, who claims to *observe* the supersensible ego in its contraction; which, in yet another parallel to the Ode, he compares to falling asleep (it should be pointed out that this is from a lecture of 1918, long before Freud's speculations were published):

> As the human being grows physically, actually his true ego slowly vanishes into the body.... His bodily nature while he is a child is

still undefined; it has as yet laid small claim to his spiritual nature, which is entering into physical existence as if it is falling asleep. (*How can Mankind Find the Christ Again?* 6)

This sounds like the way Wordsworth remembered his development, for in *The Excursion* the Wanderer speaks of "the cloud / Of infancy" in which the Creator holds "with our simplicity awhile... communion undisturbed" (4.83-86). This cloud, we may imagine, vanishes into the body over time.

The "true ego" in Steiner's spiritual taxonomy is not the transitory personality of psychoanalysis, but that part of the human being which persists over subsequent incarnations. Insofar as consciousness of it may be had, one becomes aware of the supersensible dimension of its existence.[8] This "true ego" might have its counterpart in Wordsworth's "Immortality" that "broods like the Day" over the lesser, transitory personality of the child, "a Master o'er a Slave / A Presence which is not to be put by" (119-21). Seen in these terms, the master-slave figure is not only perfectly appropriate, but somewhat disarmed of the oppressive, violent overtones that prick up the ears of critics steeped in Foucault and Marx;[9] for what evil can one possibly find in being mastered by one's immortal part? On the other hand, we have seen (p. 68, above) Steiner claim that instinctual clairvoyance had to be relinquished for mankind to free itself from deterministic spiritual forces, forces which might be figured in Wordsworth's "Presence which is not to be put by" (121). Still, we must remember that the spiritual is presented in predominantly positive terms in the Ode—"Heaven lies about us in our infancy" and the Child is "yet glorious in the might / Of heaven-born freedom" (66; 122-23)—which explains the speaker's lament for the loss of "the vision splendid."

Obstinate Questionings

In my discussion of Rudolf Steiner in chapter 3, I connected his description of the ancients' sadness before the "fallen" beauty of nature

with Wordsworth's lament of lost glory in the Ode. We saw the parallel
between the teachings of the Mysteries, that one's inner spiritual heritage
corresponds to a spirit pervading nature, and Wordsworth's consolation
from those "first affections" that spoke to him of a spirit in nature (see
page 67 above). Returning to the context of the Ode, we find that these
"first affections" are in apposition with the "obstinate questionings / Of
sense and outward things":

> Not for these I raise
> The song of thanks and praise;
> But for those obstinate questionings
> Of sense and outward things,
> Fallings from us, vanishings;
> Blank misgivings of a Creature
> Moving about in worlds not realised,
> High instincts before which our mortal Nature
> Did tremble like a guilty thing surprised:
> But for those first affections,
> Those shadowy recollections
> Which, be they what they may,
> Are yet the fountain light of all our day.... (140-152)

The "obstinate questionings" are therefore somehow connected to the
memory of the spiritual in nature that prompted "those first affections." I
suggest that the questionings refer to the mode of perception through
which Wordsworth could see the spiritual in nature.

We would find it difficult to understand how the questioning of "outward things" could possibly be consolatory if it corresponds to the
Berkeleian "idealism" expressed in the Fenwick note; some commentators
therefore propose that Wordsworth is consoled by the act of memory itself,
rather than its contents.[10] As I have argued in chapter 2, however, this "idealism" is merely a poorly-named product of a supersensible awareness

repeatedly vouchsafed in *The Prelude*. By reading the remainder of the "obstinate questionings" passage with this in mind, we find that it takes on a coherence and lucidity inaccessible with other approaches; for it continues to refer to the same lost clairvoyance that is the central theme of the poem.

Since Wordsworth once experienced the external world as "inherent in" his own "immaterial nature," it follows that the loss of this experience would make the world appear as "Fallings from us"; it has fallen away from a state of inherence. The "vanishings" apposite to these are a little more difficult to explain, however; but they do connect us back to the "something that is gone" in the first four stanzas, the celestial light that has vanished from the earth. Helen Vendler denies this connection when she accuses Trilling of confuting the light and glory of the first part of the Ode with the "vanishings" and "blank misgivings" of the second (Vendler 81-82). Apparently unable to see the possibility of a connection such as I have suggested, she concludes that "commentary falters away before this [obstinate questionings] passage, and perhaps will always fail" (82). Taking up this gauntlet, I contend that what the Ode's speaker sees as "outward things" that have fallen from us are *vanishings* from their spiritual manifestation. It is an expression remarkably appropriate by virtue of its Latin root, *evanescere*, to dissipate like vapour; for the physical objects of sense may be thought of as condensations out of the mists of spirit: "[e]verything material is condensed spirit" (Steiner, *Esoteric Development* 20). Conversely, insofar as natural objects retain a spiritual existence, they *evaporate* from physical manifestation: a process Wordsworth appears to describe when he says he was sure of his own mind as a child, while "everything else fell away, and vanished into thought" (*PW* 4.467). As Steiner avers, "[f]or the person looking into the spiritual world, the whole material, sense-perceptible world, the world in general, becomes spiritualised" (*Es. Dev.* 20) He employs the figure of dissipating vapour as well:

When a man of old saw the butterflies over the plants he saw them drawing along with them what was rising from the earth; as in an auric cloud he saw animal life flowing over the earth.

All this gradually withdrew and the prosaic world remained for man's faculty of perception which now became external.... And what man had once seen through faculties of inner perception was transformed into our modern knowledge of nature; what he had seen spiritually through faculties of external knowledge was transformed into our modern mathematics and mechanics. (*The Search for the New Isis* 37)

In Steiner's explanation, the "faculties of inner perception"—like Wordsworth's "shadowy recollections"—literally become the "master light of all our seeing," of all our science. Wordsworth, too, seems to have at least intuited this transformation by finding in "the philosophic mind" a partial recompense for the lost supersensible awareness (Ode 187).

Lest we suspect that the correspondence of Wordsworth and Steiner is too tenuously inferred from a few nebulous expressions, we might look for further support from *The Excursion*, where the Wanderer's intuitions of a prelapsarian world are much like Steiner's, flowing with "auric cloud":

> Upon the breast of new-created earth
> Man walked; and when and wheresoe'er he moved,
> Alone or mated, solitude was not.
> He heard, borne on the wind, the articulate voice
> Of God; and Angels to his sight appeared
> Crowning the glorious hills of paradise;
> Or through the groves gliding like morning mist
> Enkindled by the sun. (4.631-37)

In addition to the obvious influence of *Paradise Lost*, we find in this passage a suggestion of insubstantial angels that are more like Steiner's auric clouds than Milton's Michael. There is no suggestion in Wordsworth's passage that the "Angels" are anthropomorphic, and the metaphors he uses suggest their nebulous manifestation: they do not *stand* on the hills, they *crown* them like glories or nimbuses; they glide "like morning mist / Enkindled by the sun," which suggests a nebulous, phosphorescent manifestation as well as the manner of their motion. In fact, Wordsworth's angels are less like Milton's angels than Milton's Satan, who approaches Eden "involved in rising mist" (*PL* 9.75)—all the more reason for us to ascribe Wordsworth's description to his recollections of Edenic infancy, and not literary tradition.

"Our noisy years": Divine vs. Fallen Speech

A significant factor in the Ode-child's socialization, confinement, and loss of supersensible awareness is his acquisition of language. So long as he remains an "Eye among the blind," he is "deaf and silent" but can read "the eternal deep" (112-13): a deep which is furthermore an "eternal Silence" (156). In his gradual imprisonment on earth, on the other hand, the growing boy involves himself with imitative speech, fitting his tongue to "dialogues of business, love, or strife" (99). These, Wordsworth writes, are "our noisy years" (155). This sets up an opposition between speech and reading that, as Paul Fry notes, is reconciled only in the figure of the rolling ocean at the end of stanza 9, although Fry cannot discern "just how we are carried from sight to sound" in this stanza (68). The answer, I think, lies in an implied distinction between fallen speech, which merely signifies (or tries to signify), and divine speech that is a spiritual entity unto itself: one not only hears it, but sees, reads, or *lives* it clairvoyantly.

Although the Ode associates the loss of original clairvoyance with the acquisition of speech, this connection is much more explicit in Traherne, and we will benefit by examining its manifestation in his account first. As we saw in Traherne's autobiography, the atrophy of an "infant sensibility" was not so much a consequence of learning to speak *per se*, as of learning to think in a language that had no expressions for the supersensible world, so that all thought of that world atrophied:

> And finding no one syllable in any man's mouth of those things, by degrees they vanished, my thoughts… were blotted out; and at last all the celestial, great, and stable treasures to which I was born, as wholly forgotten, as if they had never been. (*Centuries* 157)

Traherne's "stable treasures" vanish because they are not spoken about; and perhaps because his memory has become dependent upon disinspirited language, he cannot remember his "treasures" until later in life.

For most of us, to be "deaf and silent" must appear thoroughly negative; without a concept of supersensible awareness, we must see Wordsworth's child as "lifeless" in its mute deafness (Vendler 74). For Traherne, however, these are the highest blessings:

> Wise Nature made him Deaf, too, that he might
> Not be disturbed, while he doth take Delight
> In inward Things, nor be depravd with Tongues,
> Nor Injurd by the Errors and the Wrongs
> That *Mortal Words* convey.
>
>   *   *   *   *
>
> This, my Dear friends, this was my Blessed Case;
> For nothing spoke to me but the fair Face
> Of Heav'n and Earth, before my self could speak,
> *I then my Bliss did, when my Silence, break.* ("Dumnesse" 9-20)

Here, we find evidence that not all speech is malignant; "Mortal Words" carry "Wrongs," but to be deaf to these allows one to hear "Heav'n and Earth" speaking.

In Wordsworth, the speech of Nature and infant is more felicitously characterized as *intercourse*. He captures in this term not only the sense of ordinary interlocution, but an intimacy commensurate with sexual love. Just as he is able, "by intercourse of touch," to hold "mute dialogues with [his] mother's heart" (*Prel.* 2.282-83), he could, as a child, hold

> unconscious intercourse
> With the eternal beauty, drinking in
> A pure organic pleasure from the lines
> Of curling mist, or from the level plain
> Of waters coloured by the steady clouds. (*Prelude* 1.589-93)

Although the "organic pleasure" is glossed as "bodily" by the Norton editors (60 n. 6), Wordsworth distinguishes this superadded, supersensible beauty from "vulgar joy" and "giddy bliss" a few sentences later (609-611). Insofar as he is compelled to express the intimacy of his clairvoyant intercourse with the natural world, the poet must resort to terms associated with the five senses; thus, we find him "drinking in" and gathering pleasure from fields of light "like a bee among flowers" (608). Unlike the information that comes to us through taste, however, this sensation remains an intercourse: "the earth / And common face of Nature spake to me / Rememberable things" (*Prel.* 1.614-16).[11] This intercourse or communion accords with Steiner's experience, that "in the spiritual world we sink right into whatever we perceive" (*Evolution of Consciousness* 74).

Wordsworth's diction in stanza 9 of the Ode, particularly his use of plural gerunds, may actually constitute an attempt to make fallen language more like spiritual intercourse; his nouns suggest motion, inspiration. Fred Hoerner points out that these gerunds—"questionings," "Fallings," "vanishings"—capture Wordsworth's attempt to avoid the closure of other kinds of nouns, and thus signify "processes without end" (644). I concur; by using these words, Wordsworth achieves a kind of release from the images of stasis that trouble the Ode's nadir and which are expressed in terms of "earthly freight" (127). Like Traherne's lively poetry, the very language that extinguished the child's first light becomes a breath that might rekindle the embers. Here, too, the poets accord with Steiner, who finds that it is only through words implying motion that language may approach the spiritual worlds:

> Nowadays it is exceedingly difficult to communicate with those who are in the life between death and a new birth, for the languages themselves have gradually assumed a form such as the dead no longer understand. Our nouns, for instance, soon after death, are absolute gaps in the dead man's perception of the earthly world. He only understands the verbs, the "words of time" as they are called in German—the acting, moving principle. (*Karmic Relationships* 1.48)

Wordsworth, trying to express his remembered feelings of disembodiment, appears naturally to adopt a language that Immortality will understand—even the "outward things" in stanza 9 are set in motion and become "Fall*ings* from us, vanish*ings*."

The Immortal Sea

Arguably the most powerful, most resonant passage in the Ode is the sea-shore figure that closes stanza nine:

> Though inland far we be,
> Our Souls have sight of that immortal sea
> Which brought us hither,
> Can in a moment travel thither,
> And see the Children sport upon the shore,
> And hear the mighty waters rolling evermore. (163-68)

I discussed this passage in chapter 1 as one of several examples in Wordsworth's writings where the journey of life, "beginning" in pre-existence, is mapped onto space. What is unique about the sea-shore figure is its equation of ocean and immortality. In *The Prelude*'s figure of life as an isthmus, the sense of a change of state is not as poignant, being a journey from one land to another; the immortal sea, however, becomes a place very unlike the shore of life. The figure is ideal as a vehicle for eternity, sublimity, beauty, and even the "moving principle" that Steiner finds characteristic of the spiritual world—a characteristic no less perceived by Wordsworth, who felt a presence that "rolls through all things" ("Tintern Abbey" 102). However, the "mighty waters" may be taken to signify other things as well.

Unfortunately, the ocean comes with associations of the Deluge, associations which seem to me no more pertinent to Wordsworth's design than seawater's salty taste. This has not, however, prevented several commentators from inferring a Deluge—the same commentators who imagine that the "eternal deep" read by the "Seer blest" is really some horrid abyss that Wordsworth fears rather than yearns for. Thus, Paul Fry thinks "it is only in moments of vacancy, seasons 'of calm weather,' that [Wordsworth] counteracts his fear of the eternal abyss with memories of 'sport'" (70); and Peter Manning thinks the "immortal sea" must be identical with "the apocalyptic ocean that wells up before the dreamer of *Prelude* V, the 'eternal deep' of the Ode" (92). No doubt prejudiced by the association of "God, who is our home" with the biblical Deluge, such commentators seem unwilling to posit a benevolent signification for the ocean: to posit a pre-incarnate bliss such as Wordsworth and Traherne intimated.

Rather than looking at *Prelude* 5, we ought to examine a far more relevant passage from *The Excursion*, in which the "ethereal deep" is an unmistakably benevolent *Heaven*. Wordsworth describes the state of Adam "Upon the breast of new-created earth":

[Man] sate—and talked
With winged Messengers; who daily brought
To his small island in the ethereal deep
Tidings of joy and love. (4.638-41)

Here, all of material existence is a "small island in the ethereal deep": an eternal deep, antedating the flood, out of which only "[t]idings of joy and love" are brought. If we choose not to ignore this passage, and read it as a gloss on the Ode, the sea-shore figure is potentially freed from all association with the Deluge, and the palpable transport in Wordsworth's expression becomes fitting.

The relationship between the children on the shore and this "eternal deep" is also a matter requiring some elucidation. To Cleanth Brooks, the importance of their juxtaposition is to show that children are close to immortality and its wisdom by virtue of their sporting: "they are playing with their little spades and sand-buckets along the beach on which the waves break" (143). Of course, none of this is found in the poem, other than the word "sport," and Brooks duly excuses himself for making the passage appear bathetic. In fact, to suggest that the children are closer to God through their play is to ignore the first half of the stanza, where Wordsworth tells us he does not mean to praise "Delight and liberty, the simple creed / Of Childhood" (137-38). The relationship of child and immortality is rather one of intimate communion or intercourse which, as we have seen, Wordsworth mentions often. The poet's illustration of this communion in the sea-shore figure is perhaps connected to his Sonnet, "It is a beauteous evening," and the meeting with his daughter that inspired it:

The gentleness of heaven broods o'er the Sea:
Listen! the mighty Being is awake,
And doth with his eternal motion make
A sound like thunder—everlastingly.
Dear Child! dear girl! that walkest with me here,

If thou appear untouched by solemn thought,
Thy nature is not therefore the less divine:
Thou liest in Abraham's bosom all the year;
And worshipp'st at the Temple's inner shrine,
God being with thee when we know it not. (lines 5-14)

The correspondences between this Sonnet, written in 1802, and the Immortality Ode are remarkable: both poems mention the motion, sound, and eternity of the ocean; both refer to a "brooding" entity; and both make a distinction between the adult soul's occasional visit(ation)s of the eternal, and the child's *residence* "in Abraham's bosom." This residence is illustrated in the sea-shore figure, where the children may be imagined as half-immersed in the immortal sea at times.

This is certainly how Elizabeth Barrett Browning read stanza 9; the unmistakable allusion to it in *Aurora Leigh* shows her appreciation of the pre-existence theme behind it:

I, writing thus, am still what men call young;
I have not so far left the coasts of life
To travel inward, that I cannot hear
That murmur of the outer Infinite
Which unweaned babies smile at in their sleep
When wondered at for smiling.... (1.9-14)

Although it is Aurora speaking, and we need not suspect Barrett Browning of sharing Wordsworth's recollections, the fact that she, too, takes pre-existence seriously is indicated in the infant's smile, by which she alludes to Thomas Taylor's evidence for pre-existence:

[I]nfants are not seen to laugh for nearly three weeks after birth, but pass the greatest part of this time in sleep; however, in their sleep they are often seen both to laugh and cry. But how is it possible that

this can otherwise happen than through the soul being agitated by
the whirling motions of the animal nature, and moved in conform-
ity to the passions which it had experienced in another life?[12]

In "A Child Asleep," Barrett Browning devotes a full poem to this idea,
while alluding constantly to the Immortality Ode:

> Shapes of brightness overlean thee,
>   Flash their diadems of youth
> In the ringlets which half screen thee,
>   While thou smilest . . not in sooth
> *Thy* smile, but the overfair one, dropt from some aetherial mouth.
>
>   *   *   *   *
>
> Softly, softly! make no noises!
>   Now he lieth dead and dumb;
> Now he hears the angels' voices
>   Folding silence in the room:
> Now he muses deep the meaning of the Heaven-words as
> they come.
>
>   (31-45)

Judging by the interpretations implicit in her borrowings from the
Ode, I think we would be justified in assuming that Barrett Browning
read the Ode much as we have read it: as *intimations of immortality* (and
pre-incarnation) *from recollections of early childhood.*

The Consolation

As I have argued, the consolatory force of stanzas 9-11 of the Ode is
somewhat greater than it would appear if we did not take pre-existence
and supersensible awareness seriously; Wordsworth's memory of the spiritual presence in nature mitigates his feeling of estrangement, while the

recollection of pre-existence brings faith in immortality. I say faith, for it is not clear that Wordsworth has achieved the certainty of a Socrates in this matter; he may remain at the stage of Cebes, who in the *Phaedo* was at first in doubt whether the soul might yet be perishable, even if it outlived a number of incarnations (86a-88b).

Nor am I certain that Wordsworth achieves the expression of continuity and unity hoped for in the 1815 epigraph: "And I could wish my days to be / Bound each to each by natural piety." As Manning observes, there is too much "pathos of change and separation" in the Ode for it to live up to this wish (94). But this pathos does not necessarily imply the kind of *psychomachia* inferred by Daniel Ross, for example, who thinks Wordsworth "confronts the child as a threat" (626). I think the kind of division he experiences is better compared to that of one who feels that his dream-consciousness, though different from waking, is nevertheless part of himself; when the memory of this dream-life fades "into the light of common day," however, one seldom experiences it as a rupture of psychic integrity. Only the most exalted, most beautiful dreams leave one with the sense that "there hath past away a glory from the earth," and even the loss of these is to some extent mitigated by our enjoyment of a fuller consciousness. By afternoon, we may feel strength in hours "that bring the philosophic mind," and feel revived by the winds that come to us "from the fields of sleep"; as we watch the "Clouds that gather round the setting sun," we may feel consoled that another day hath been—"and other palms are won."

As the poet himself says of his communion with nature, "a Reader who has not a vivid recollection of these feelings having existed in his mind cannot understand" the Ode.[13] If Wordsworth is, in fact, talking about a history of extrovertive mystical experience or supersensible perception, this places most of us at a great disadvantage as readers. As I have shown, however, we can examine the testimony of others who claim to have had similar experiences in order to clarify to ourselves that which remains vague in Wordsworth. We can also try to exercise our imagination and sympathize with the poet's experience: a way of reading which, as I argue in the following chapters, is wanting in much commentary on the Ode since the time of Coleridge.

Chapter 5

The Immortality Ode vs. Coleridge and Religious Orthodoxy

> The continued recommendation of the
> *Biographia* as a sympathetic and authoritative
> introduction to Wordsworth can only tend to
> confuse and alienate.
> —Richard Gravil, "Coleridge's Wordsworth" 38

Whether or not the reader is willing to take the notion of pre-existence seriously, I think that I have made it clear that Wordsworth probably did take it seriously. I have also sought to show how a reading of the Immortality Ode that accepts Wordsworth's credulity avoids many of the difficulties that have vitiated commentary on the Ode. Such a reading might also reconstruct the response of some early applauders for whom the poem was the "divinest utterance of modern poetry,"[1] and, as in the case of Elizabeth Barrett Browning, for whom it was worthy of imitation. I submit that my approach has therefore always been available, at least insofar as it examines Wordsworth apart from Traherne, Chamberlain, and Steiner; that it consistently has been avoided, however, I find indicative of critics' prejudice against the ideas of pre-existence and supersensible perception. This prejudice is nowhere more evident than in Coleridge, for whom, as we shall see, it was a distinctly *religious* prejudice, even though it was expressed and received in terms of aesthetic criticisms.

Coleridge's attack on the Immortality Ode in *Biographia Literaria* is legendary, and traces of it appear in subsequent commentary almost as much as allusions to the Ode itself. Furthermore, it comes in a book that, as Mark Edmundson would have it, "lays the foundation for Anglo-American philosophical criticism by providing a systematic method for describing and evaluating poetry" (741): a book that Thomas Raysor called "the finest critical essay in English literature" ("Coleridge's Criticism of Wordsworth" 497). Yet if one accepts the kind of exegesis I have engaged in, it becomes clear that Coleridge is not interested in sympathetically engaging the parts of the Ode that he singles out for the most intense criticism: stanzas 5 and 8, the passages on incarnation and the panegyric on the child. I. A. Richards notes Coleridge's "inattentive, unresponsive and unresourceful reading" as well (130), but fails to see what is more pernicious: these criticisms, as well as Coleridge's subsequent elision of them, stem from doctrinal preconceptions that are not easily discerned. As I shall demonstrate, Coleridge is averse to the idea of pre-existence, an aversion which leads him to interpret the doctrine's appearance as metaphoric; furthermore, he is averse to mysticism—at least in his maturity—and therefore upbraids his friend for speaking like an enthusiast. I would argue that both aversions are basically religious, and proceed from Coleridge's effort to establish himself as a *bona fide* Trinitarian and Anglican.[2]

To some extent, however, Coleridge's objections can be traced to his inability to see that Wordsworth draws his panegyric on the child from self-observation. After demanding why we should regard a child as a philosopher, and positing a few mocking responses, Coleridge concludes that knowledge of such precocious sagacity is in any case inaccessible to adult observers:

> In what sense is he declared to be "*for ever haunted* by the Supreme Being? or so inspired as to deserve the splendid titles of a *mighty prophet*, a *blessed seer*? By reflection? by knowledge? by conscious intuition? or by *any* form or modification of consciousness?" These would be tidings indeed; but such as would pre-suppose an immediate revelation to the inspired communicator, and require miracles to authenticate his inspiration. Children at this age give no such information of themselves…. (*BL* 2.138)

As I have shown, and as the variants discovered by Curtis clearly bear out,[3] Wordsworth requires no other revelation than his own memory to "authenticate" these tidings; the memories themselves may be questioned on other grounds, but we need not demand "miracles" to authenticate them. Wordsworth may be accused of generalizing his experience without making it clear that he is doing so; yet this is so typical of Wordsworth that we must lay some blame upon Coleridge for failing to see this case as an instance of Wordsworth's habitual mode of thought. Furthermore, Coleridge might have looked at the extended, 1815 title, which clarifies the source of Wordsworth's assertions: "Ode: Intimations of Immortality from Recollections of Early Childhood." One begins to wonder whether Coleridge is blinded by something else.

Another justifiable criticism seems to derive from Wordsworth's conflation of the personal and the general, namely that no one appears to recall this blessed childhood: as Coleridge puts it, "At what time were we dipped in the Lethe, which has produced such utter oblivion of a state so godlike?"

(*BL* 2.138-39). Coleridge tries to answer for Wordsworth, suggesting that perhaps "these mysterious gifts, faculties, and operations are *not* accompanied by consciousness"; but he finds this explanation most unsatisfactory because it raises the question, "who *else* is conscious of them?" (2.139). Again, the problem proceeds from Wordsworth's generalization, but one intuits that Coleridge cannot even imagine that Wordsworth may be speaking from experience rather than speculation. As we have seen, Wordsworth *does* have recollections—be they what they may—of a childhood state akin to that of a prophet or seer, as he repeatedly avers in *The Prelude*. One need only recall Plato's *Republic* to understand his idiosyncrasy in mythical terms; Wordsworth's baptism "in the Lethe"—just prior to birth in the myth of Er[4]—was, perhaps, incomplete. Because Coleridge, like most of us, did not share the experience that this explanatory fiction refers to, he can only imagine that Wordsworth implies that the memory is lost, in *all* cases, at precisely the age when we acquire the ability to communicate it. But the possibility of variation in human psychology should be obvious: as Coleridge says elsewhere, and ought to have remembered had he been less preoccupied with castigating Wordsworth, "the analogy between death and sleep is... natural":[5] we are dipped in the Lethe every time we wake up in the morning; some of us remember our dreams quite well, some only vaguely, and some not at all.

The myth of Er ought also to have occurred to Coleridge, who was familiar with Plato and many Neoplatonists. But the theme of pre-existence in Plato was something that he would have liked to forget; after announcing that Wordsworth does not believe in pre-existence, Coleridge appends the stupefying avowal, that he does not believe "that Plato himself ever meant or taught it" (2.147). This would indicate that he either thinks Plato does not endorse the teachings of Socrates—an opinion, I think, no one could defend—or that Coleridge wilfully ignores important passages of the *Meno*, *Republic*, and *Phaedrus*, as well as the most important part of the *Phaedo*:

> SOCRATES: Then if there *is* such a thing as coming to life again,
> wouldn't this, coming to life again, be a process from dead to liv-
> ing people?
> CEBES: Certainly.
> SOCRATES: In that way too, then, we're agreed that living people
> are born from the dead no less than dead people from the living;
> and we thought that, if this were the case, it would be sufficient
> evidence that the souls of the dead must exist somewhere, whence
> they are born again. (*Phaedo* 71e-72a)

In the *Phaedo*, pre-existence is a given from which immortality is
argued; in the *Phaedrus*, it is a given from which a theory of desire is
argued; in the *Meno*, where *anamnesis* is argued. To doubt that Plato ever
"meant or taught" pre-existence seems to me absurd, and indicative of
prejudices that—as shall soon be made clear—Coleridge contracts from
the given doctrines of the Church of England.

What makes his denial particularly bizarre is Coleridge's acknowledge-
ment, albeit twenty years earlier, that Plato *does* mean and teach pre-existence. In a sonnet appearing originally in a Letter to Poole, and
subsequently to Thelwall, Coleridge toys with the idea of pre-existence
himself and refers it to Plato:

> Oft of some *Unknown Past* such fancies roll
> Swift o'er my brain, as make the Present seem,
> For a brief moment, like a most strange Dream
> When, not unconscious that [s]he dreamt, the Soul
> Questions herself in sleep: and Some have said
> We liv'd ere yet this *fleshly* robe we wore.[6]

In an effort to assure his correspondent that he is not serious about this
"wild Philosophy" (*Letters* 1.278), Coleridge glosses the "fleshly robe we
wore" as "alluding to Plato's doc[trine] of pre-existence." Furthermore, in

the published, 1797 version of the sonnet, he acknowledges the doctrine's appearance in the *Phaedo* by quoting Cebes' avowal of pre-existence as a footnote (Chayes 291). Somewhere between 1797 and 1817, then, his opinion of Plato's teaching had undergone a radical transformation.

One of the intervening developments, of course, was Coleridge's acceptance of Anglicanism and the belief in the Trinity that this entailed. As Mary Anne Perkins points out, this conversion was partially effected through Plato's conception of the Logos:

> The Logos became the cause of Coleridge's rejection of Unitarianism, the means by which he was finally able 'to reconcile personality with infinity' (*BL* i. 201) and by which the philosophical acceptance of triunity was transformed into Trinitarian faith in a God who revealed himself in the Person of the Logos who is Christ. (16)

The connection of Platonic triunity to Trinitarianism is especially important since Coleridge saw the Trinity as an idea of God "which rescues our faith from both extremes, Cabalo-Pantheism, and Anthropomorphism";[7] Plato, therefore, led him away from the Spinozas, mystics, and enthusiasts he had read in his youth,[8] many of which—most notably Plotinus and Proclus—zealously proclaimed the doctrine of pre-existence. We can therefore safely assume that his doubt of Plato's commitment to pre-existence arose from Coleridge's desire to preserve the philosopher as a route to Trinitarian Christianity. Insofar as Plato's teaching of pre-existence led back in the direction of heterodoxy, it became something to be denied; insofar as pre-existence in Wordsworth's Ode led in the direction of heterodoxy, this became something to be denied all the more, for it raised the issue of Plato's pre-existence all over again.

That Coleridge was quite inquisitorial in defending his new-found faith against the encroachments of "Cabalo-Pantheism" is evident in one of the *Philosophical Lectures* of 1819. After first desynonymizing

Platonism and Plotinism—a difference we might compare to that obtaining between Anglicans and Puritans—Coleridge explains how the latter "seems to have been unfavourable to the Reformation" on account of its mysticism (*Lectures* 317). He then waxes apocalyptic about the effect of these "other" Platonisms on the continent:

> Even to this day the far greater number of converts to the Romish Church, among the educated class, are drawn into it by the attractive PIETISM in that church...that attracted our CRASHAW. And the revised PROCLO-PLOTINISM EVEN AT THIS VERY HOUR IS MULTIPLYING NOMINAL CATHOLICS AMONG THE YOUNG MEN THROUGHOUT GERMANY.[9]

Proclus and Plotinus are particularly important targets for Coleridge, being closely associated with Plato and, perhaps, dangerously popular among the "educated class" in England on account of Thomas Taylor's translations. Taylor's 1816 translation of Proclus must have been particularly difficult for Coleridge to stomach: the English title became *Proclus, the Platonic Successor, on The Theology of Plato.* Nor would Coleridge's antipathy have been isolated: as Kathleen Raine points out, Taylor incurred the wrath of the *Edinburgh Review,* which attacked him for "exhibiting Plato as the mortal foe both of reason, and of taste" by associating Plato with Proclus.[10] Through Thomas Taylor and Proclus, Platonism becomes a rival instead of the ally of established religion that Coleridge found. Thus, "Proclo-Platonism" becomes a matter of heresy instead of philosophy, and Coleridge feels he must defend Wordsworth against the "charge" of believing the "platonic pre-existence in the ordinary interpretation of the words," as though Wordsworth were on trial for heresy (*BL* 2.147). Instead of wondering to what extent Coleridge caused the appearance of pre-existence in the Ode—as criticism has done at least since Rea in 1928—we should perhaps wonder to what extent he *prevented* its appearance in Wordsworth's other works.

An orthodox rehabilitation of Wordsworth would have become inconsequential for further criticism had it been more explicit; commentators could have noted and compensated for it. But Coleridge goes about it in such a way that this rehabilitation appears to become an issue of exegesis divorced from doctrine:

> The Ode was intended for such readers only as had been accustomed to watch the flux and reflux of their inmost nature, to venture at times into the twilight realms of consciousness, and to feel a deep interest in modes of inmost being, to which they know that the attributes of time and space are inapplicable and alien.... For such readers the sense is sufficiently plain, and they will be as little disposed to charge Mr. Wordsworth with believing the platonic pre-existence in the ordinary interpretation of the words, as I am to believe, that Plato himself ever meant or taught it. (2.147)

The implication, of course, is that if we insist on thinking Wordsworth and Plato are serious about pre-existence, we cannot belong to Coleridge's elite school of introspection.[11] Furthermore, it is up to us to disabuse ourselves of "the ordinary interpretation of the words" to gain full access to Plato and Wordsworth. Coleridge in effect invites us to read like the early Christian mythographers: to intentionally misread works arising from another culture and worldview to support the beliefs of a contemporary orthodoxy. The hermeneutics advocated by Fulgentius (c. 450?) might be taken as a precursor of Coleridge's imperative:

> What I wish to do is to expose alterations away from the truth, not obscure what is clear by altering it myself.... I look for the true effects of things, whereby, once the fictional invention of lying Greeks has been disposed of, I may infer what allegorical significance one should understand in such matters. (17)

"The allegorical significance one should understand" inevitably conforms to Christian morality in Fulgentius's mythography; thus the polytheism of "lying Greeks" is suppressed by making their myths speak for orthodoxy.

It appears, then, that Coleridge suppresses the Ode's heterodox doctrine at least partly out of an impulse to defend Wordsworth against the "charge" of believing it. Yet this remains a case in which pre-emptive acquittal does not erase suspicion, and may even create it. Furthermore, Coleridge's acquittal of Wordsworth comes only after he finds him guilty of another heresy: the objections to the panegyric on the child are not only motivated by misunderstanding, but by Coleridge's desire to show that the prophetic strains of stanza 8 are founded on mystical illusions such as he came to equate with *enthusiasm*.

We have seen how Coleridge linked mysticism and pre-existence in what he called "Proclo-Plotinism," which was "unfavorable to the Reformation"; in *Aids to Reflection*, he draws upon the rationalist arguments of Locke to make a further link between mysticism and enthusiasm:

> The grounding of any theory or belief on accidents and anomalies of individual sensations or fancies, and the use of peculiar terms invented or perverted from their ordinary significations, for the purpose of expressing these *idiosyncrasies*, and pretended facts of interior consciousness, I name Mysticism. Where the error consists simply in the Mystic's attaching to these anomalies of his individual temperament the character of *Reality*, and in receiving them as Permanent Truths,... I should regard it as a species of Enthusiasm, always indeed to be deprecated, but yet capable of co-existing with many excellent qualities both of Head and Heart.[12]

Thus, anyone who claims to perceive something different from others ("pretended facts of interior consciousness") and tries to expand the use of language to describe these perceptions, is potentially a mystic and enthusiast, "always indeed to be deprecated." Insofar as Coleridge held a similar view of mystics when, six years earlier, he wrote the *Biographia*, we must wonder whether there is any value in his praise of Wordsworth's powers when he appears to credit his friend with a healthy mysticism:

> For without his depth of feeling and his imaginative power his *Sense* would want its vital warmth and peculiarity; and without his strong sense, his *mysticism* would become *sickly*—mere fog, and dimness! (2.142)

Since this passage concludes the lengthy exposition of Wordsworth's *lack* of sense in parts of the Ode, we can only surmise that Coleridge not only thought his former friend an enthusiast, but not a very good enthusiast at that; lacking even the moonlight that "gives to all objects a tender visionary hue and softening," as Coleridge describes the mystic's experience (*AR* 393)—without even this, Wordsworth is mere fog, mere clouds: *evanescens*.

Returning to Coleridge's expostulations over the child-philosopher, we discover that he in fact applies to Wordsworth the same philosophical machinery that Locke uses against enthusiasm and the nonconformist sects that this term once blanketed. Coleridge states that any claim to knowledge of unique childhood faculties "would presuppose an immediate revelation to the inspired communicator, and require miracles to authenticate"—an echo, I think, of Locke's distinction between revelations that are really just strong "persuasions" (enthusiasm), and biblical revelations supposedly attended by miracles and therefore as good as reason (*Essay* 4.19.11-15). But Coleridge's first subtle charge of enthusiasm is not sufficient. He moves on to suggest that if the Child is godlike by virtue of its existing as a part of the being of God, Wordsworth might be a pantheist (another species of enthusiast), and not a very good one at that; even pantheists like Spinoza and Böhme, he proclaims, "would not confound the *part*, *as* a part, with the Whole, *as* the whole" (*BL* 2.139).

Unspent after this insinuation, he wonders if Wordsworth dubs the child "best Philosopher" because it appears, in the grave passage, to think of death as "lying in a dark, cold place"—the kind of perverse belief only an enthusiast could hold.[13]

Ultimately Coleridge seems to decide he must extricate Wordsworth from these charges of heterodoxy and stupidity, by once again telling us we must learn to read more subtly to overcome the "splendid paradoxes" we encounter in a text:

> Thus you must at once understand the words *contrary* to their common import, in order to arrive at any *sense*; and *according* to their common import, if you are to receive from them any feeling of *sublimity* or *admiration*. (1.141)

This formula concludes Coleridge's negative commentary on the Ode, perhaps as a final suggestion to help readers who discover the "splendid paradox" that John Mathison, writing in 1949, finds in the Ode: "[h]ow can we enjoy a poem which, we are sure, is nonsense?" (419). For Mathison, as for many New and Newer Critics, the answer lay in blindly following Coleridge into a world of "splendid paradoxes" where "you must... understand the words *contrary* to their common import, in order to arrive at any sense": a world where the issue of pre-existence in the Ode is elided by calling it a mere metaphor, an empty signifier, an unnecessary hypothesis:

> It is the supposed necessity of defending passages as always true, or as part of the poet's settled view of things, not as particularly appropriate, that has caused the trouble. Actually, before the conclusion, the hypothesis becomes unnecessary to the general thought of the poem, having fulfilled its function in vivifying the memory, but it remains an integral part of the reverie, and it is the bridge which gets the poem from "sullenness" to understanding. (Mathison 439)

Of course Wordsworth only contributes to this evisceration of signifi-cance when he calls pre-existence a mere "Archimedean point" on which he rested the machinery of his poem (Fenwick note); and one wonders if even he had begun to see the social expediency of re-presenting his poem in Coleridge's terms.

Following Coleridge

Although we might discern in Coleridge the roots of New Critical approaches to the Ode (and perhaps poetry in general), the religious tinc-ture of Coleridge's prejudice is eventually replaced by what I shall call a positivistic prejudice, which I shall examine in chapter 6. The religious does not disappear, however; it slowly blends into the positivistic, just as the voice of High Church Toryism blends so easily with the incipient pos-itivism of John Locke in his discussion "Of Enthusiasm" (4.19.1ff).

Mathison's approach to the Ode is actually a good example of this blending process. When he says that the poem is "nonsense," it is not immediately clear whether he means it does not accord with *revelation*, or does not accord with *reason*. This ambiguity is even better exemplified as he begins his exegesis:

> I would like to examine the section beginning with stanza five, in its setting in the poem, to see if the context does not have an important qualifying effect on the stanzas, and help to account for the fact that actually we do not object while we are reading the poem to a passage we should never subscribe to as an ordinary statement of belief. (434)

The approach sounds very scientific, but if we read from the point of view of someone who *does* subscribe to pre-existence—a Hindu, Buddhist, or Christian who happens to believe in reincarnation, for example—the religious prejudice becomes obvious. We would have to wonder: does the critic approach *Paradise Lost* in the same way? If the incarnation account in the Ode is rejected on scientific grounds, why do we not reject Milton's creation account also, and ask why we still enjoy it? Mathison does not make his religious prejudices explicit (he may indeed be unaware of them, in which case we might call them cultural prejudices), but they are easily inferred. Their consequence, as we have seen in Coleridge, is the creation of a hermeneutical problem from which we can never really escape unless we admit that it need not be a problem: Wordsworth probably believed in pre-existence when he wrote the Ode, so one needn't worry about explaining the lines away. As for the reason Mathison can enjoy the poem while rejecting pre-existence utterly, we can only speculate whether, by some unconscious *anamnesis*, the lines do not ring true for him after all.—But I should rather attribute it to the now atavistic enjoyment that most men once automatically derived from all canonized texts, the enjoyment that arises from knowing that readers in the past have, for whatever reason, enjoyed the same texts.

A few commentators are much more candid about recuperating a reading of the Ode that accords with certain Christian orthodoxies. As we have seen, Coleridge adumbrates the possibility of reading the Ode in such a way that we will not charge Wordsworth with believing in pre-existence, and some critics have followed these indications by reading the Ode-child's incarnation allegorically. This is the approach taken in 1978 by James Pipkin, for whom the poem is a secularization of "Biblical myth," namely the myth of the fall:

> Wordsworth turns in the Ode to traditional theological concepts, imagery, and design, and finds inherent in his own experience the Christian pattern of the fall, the redemption, and the restored paradise. (91)

In order to make such a claim, of course, the untraditional theological concept of the Ode-child's loss of pre-existent and perinatal glory must be read as a type of the Fall, at the expense of any literal level of signification. Since the loss of this glory conveys "the idea of separateness or division," Pipkin feels justified in claiming that the loss "reflect[s] the most basic element in the traditional concept of the Fall" (Pipkin 91). The implication here is that anything that conveys "the idea of separateness or division," and therefore almost any heterodox writing, is translatable into the myth of the Fall. But even before taking this step, Pipkin introduces the authority of the poet and the Fenwick note to justify his allegorical approach:

> [Wordsworth] grounds his explanation in his memories of childhood experiences, but he supports much of what he says by referring to the Bible. He recalls brooding over the stories of Enoch and Elijah, and after granting that there is no direct evidence "in revelation" of a prior state of existence, he proposes that "the fall of man presents an analogy in its favor." (91)

I think Wordsworth means to say that perhaps the account of the Fall in the bible is a mythological representation of pre-existence (albeit on a racial scale), and not the other way around; he is defending the doctrine as potentially orthodox by presenting the "fall of man" as "an analogy in its favor," *not* suggesting a way of reading his poem allegorically. Guided by religious (or cultural) prejudice, however, Pipkin reads the signs of orthodoxy in the Fenwick note instead of the subtle defence of pre-existence.[14]

David Rogers, on the other hand, avoids the difficulty of reducing Wordsworth's incarnation passage to a Fall narrative by deciding that pre-existence is entirely superfluous to the poem. In "God and Pre-existence in Wordsworth's Immortality Ode," an article of 1969, Rogers attempts to minimize the importance of pre-existence by comparing it to the importance of God:

> Since the idea of pre-existence depends upon and is subordinate to the idea of God as origin and ultimate home of the soul, it cannot be the philosophical basis of the poem. In short, the idea that God is the origin and final resting place of the soul is far more important for the poem than whether our souls existed before their actual birth into time. If the idea of pre-existence were left out of the poem its intellectual structure would suffer no serious damage. (143)

Not surprisingly, Rogers never demonstrates how the "intellectual structure" of the poem remains intact by eviscerating the main idea of stanza 5. The rest of his article is devoted to showing how Wordsworth *really did* believe in God, as though the possibility that he believed in pre-existence might somehow preclude this. Rogers draws upon the evidence of the Fenwick note to make his case but is content to cite only Wordsworth's protestation against his intention "to inculcate" belief in pre-existence; Wordsworth's qualifications and defence of the doctrine Rogers conveniently ignores. All of this evidence, he concludes, is not supported *by*, but rather "supports Coleridge's comment in the *Biographia*" that an elite of subtle readers will not charge Wordsworth with believing in pre-existence. And

> [s]urely Coleridge, who had discussed the idea with Wordsworth and who was the poet's best friend at the time of the poem's com-position, knew the sense in which he accepted the idea for use in the 'Ode'.

The "he" in "he accepted the idea" belies the critic's presumption: we might take the pronoun to refer to Coleridge, in which case Rogers tells us that Coleridge "knew the sense in which [Coleridge] accepted the idea for use in the 'Ode'." This "sense" also happens to be the sense in which Rogers accepts it. By following the authority of Coleridge so closely, he cannot even begin to explore an alternative reading, and he certainly gives us no new insight into the poem.

Not all of the twentieth-century critics follow Coleridge precisely in this manner, however. Others are more concerned with attacking the poem's visionary passages, and I am sure Gerald Solomon is not unique in taking up the stick of enthusiasm with which Coleridge rapped Wordsworth in the *Biographia*. In "Wordsworth and 'the Art of Lying'," Solomon continues where Coleridge's negative criticism left off, portraying Wordsworth as a muddle-headed enthusiast.

At first, Solomon's attack is carried out under the pretense of philosophical criticisms such as Coleridge began with:

> In an attempt to support the primary demands of his fantasies [Wordsworth] went behind the back, so to speak, of his own better judgement. He resorted, unconsciously, to fallacies of thinking (paralogisms) and fallacies of perceiving (hallucinations). (146)

Without examining the propriety of defining hallucinations as "fallacies in perceiving"—fallacies being matters of logic, not perception—we must wonder what the critic means when he says Wordsworth "resorted, unconsciously." It appears that we must apply Coleridge's rules for dealing with "splendid paradoxes" here (which, incidentally, Solomon quotes at the beginning of his article): by "he resorted," Solomon implies a willful and obviously sinister agency that goes "behind the back"; by "unconsciously," he implies that Wordsworth was yet the toy of irrational desires. On both counts, the image of the sinister, irrational enthusiast begins to construct itself.

Although Solomon begins by outlining the "confusion" about death in the Immortality Ode, it is in his analysis of the "Beauteous Evening" sonnet that he exemplifies his failure to make any sense of the concept of the soul that we have traced in Wordsworth. The sonnet, which I connected to the Ode in chapter 4, has a father addressing his child as "Thou [who]

liest in Abraham's bosom all the year"—that is, addressing her as still connected to the spiritual world, still on the shore of incarnation. For
Solomon, however, the line amounts to a suppressed wish of the father to
see his daughter dead:

> There are sinister implications in Wordsworth's fantasy. By
> despatching his daughter to Abraham's bosom he could be seen as
> sending her as an innocent and fit emissary to the Heaven he has
> set his heart on. But in order to do this, he would have to, as it
> were, 'kill' her. A painful situation would result, whereby in
> 'killing' Anne-Caroline, Wordsworth would also be renewing for
> himself the experience of the child left deserted by the parents....
> (We are, of course, considering fantasies, not actual performances,
> so moral conclusions at this stage would be out of place.) (149)

Sensing, perhaps, that his exegesis is turning into a trial, Solomon
inserts the parenthetical disclaimer after convicting the poet of murderous
intentions: a strategy of *accuse, smear* irrevocably, and *acquit* that he seems
to have learned from Coleridge. But one cannot credit him with having
achieved Coleridge's subtlety:

> Wordsworth reveals in his deliberated yet irrational image [i.e.,
> Abraham's bosom] the nature of his underlying fantasy-wishes,
> and the state of his mind when composing such poetry....
> Moreover, it seems that rational control of expression is subverted
> and impaired, not only to further the designs of the unconscious
> mind, but also perhaps to exult in a liberation from conscious
> control such as is enjoyed by the drug addict, to be an enthusiast
> for enthusiasm's sake.... (148)

A curious composite of all that Solomon finds evil begins to emerge:
the somewhat anachronistic "enthusiast," that blanket term for dissenters

who claimed revelations from God, becomes linked with "drug addict," a particularly resonant term in the 1970s, when the article appeared.

But Solomon does not stop here; he implies a connection to Wordsworth's early affiliations with France as well:

> ...to be an enthusiast for enthusiasm's sake, to escape the common-sense approach which threatens to make him 'dull... of soul'. In another sonnet written at the same time, Wordsworth noted with approval the fervour of revolutionary France: 'The senselessness of joy was then sublime!' (149)

Although it is not made explicit why this statement about revolutionary France is particularly relevant, its significance is indicated by its proximity to "enthusiasm for enthusiasm's sake": we are meant to see that Wordsworth's irrationalism is of a piece with revolutionary fervour and religious nonconformism—all that opposes Anglican rationalism. In this respect, Solomon's rhetoric differs little from a parallel passage in Edmund Burke's *Reflections on the Revolution in France*:

> If, in the moment of riot, and in a drunken delirium from the hot spirit drawn out of the alembick of hell, which in France is now so furiously boiling, we should uncover our nakedness by throwing off that Christian religion which has hitherto been... one great source of civilization amongst us, and among many other nations, we are apprehensive (being well aware that the mind will not endure a void) that some uncouth, pernicious, and degrading superstition, might take the place of it. (1285)

If Solomon, in 1977, can exhibit traces of Burke's eighteenth-century prejudice, we should not be surprised to discover Solomon's critical ancestor in Coleridge, and Coleridge's ancestor in Fulgentius.

It has not been my intent to suggest that Anglicans, Christians, or other religious readers are necessarily poor or prejudiced exegetes. Confronted with Donne's sonnets, or even Wordsworth's *Ecclesiastical Sonnets*, I would expect readers committed to Anglicanism among the most elucidative. What I hope to have made clear by exploring the effect of religious prejudice on the Ode is the blindness or deceitfulness of those who pretend to interpret scientifically while exercising prejudice, and those who criticize logic and aesthetics when they mean to dispute doctrine. Such pretenses are by no means confined to what I have called religious readers. As I have suggested, religious prejudice is largely replaced by positivistic prejudice in the twentieth century, but not before it constructs a critical mindset wherein the issue of pre-existence continues to be ignored, translated into something entirely different, or attacked as inconsistent with the proper worldview of the day.

Chapter 6

The Immortality Ode vs.
Positivistic Orthodoxy

Just as Coleridge tried to suppress the doctrine of pre-existence to preserve the appearance of Wordsworth's (and Plato's) religious orthodoxy, some later commentators have tried to suppress it to save the Ode for a positivist orthodoxy that treats any claim of disembodied consciousness, even in poetry, as a pernicious lie. Some, such as John Stuart Mill, have looked for ways of redeeming the Ode as poetry while discarding the philosophy of pre-existence that vitiates it, while other commentators, following the reading strategies of the allegorical critics, have tried to translate the Ode into scientific language and ideas. Although I would be foolish not to respect the opinion of those who reject pre-existence as a philosophical postulate, I think we are justified in finding these readers prejudiced when they try to force a reading of their worldview onto a poem that will not support it or even manifestly contradicts it, or when they apply to pre-existence a standard of truth that is suspended in evaluations of Dante, Homer, or even Wordsworth's more orthodox theological poems. The double standard thus invoked might, as I have suggested, be more properly termed a cultural prejudice, but since it appears under the pretence of scientific language and methods, I shall continue to call it positivistic prejudice.

As M. H. Abrams notes in "Belief and Disbelief," the strictures of positivism presented a challenge to all poetry in the nineteenth century. Abrams cites Jeremy Bentham as the champion of this movement, along with John Stuart Mill as a conciliatory negotiator:

> Bentham, heir to the traditional English semantics of scientific language, charged that by the standards of "logical truth" poetic statements are false.... John Stuart Mill, a disciple of Bentham's who became an ardent defender of poetry, although in terms controlled by the semantics of positivism, defined poetry as "the expression or uttering forth of feeling," and therefore what he called the "logical opposite" of "matter of fact or science." (118-19)

Mill, of course, bases his definition on Wordsworth, who wrote in his Preface to *Lyrical Ballads* that poetry is the "spontaneous overflow of powerful feelings" (*PW* 2.400). But Mill ignores Wordsworth's other statements about poetry, namely that it may express even the most serious "matter of fact": "[t]he remotest discoveries of the Chemist, the Botanist, or Mineralogist, will be as proper objects of the Poet's art as any upon which it can be employed..." (*PW* 2.396-97). The oversight is convenient, if not planned, for it allows Mill to confront Wordsworth's statements in the Immortality Ode not as observations, but as poetic illusions, "conception[s] known not to be true" that nonetheless extract "the same benefit to the feelings which would be derived from [them] if [they] were a reality."[1] Whether or not the poet's statements are based on observations may remain impossible to prove, but Mill would prevent us from even considering them thus.

I think it is no accident that Mill's formulation echoes Coleridge's discussion of "splendid paradoxes" in *Biographia Literaria* (see page 105-06, above). Just as Coleridge had to propose a hermeneutic to absolve Plato and Wordsworth of religious heterodoxy, Mill needed a way to reconcile his positivism with a love and respect for Wordsworth, and for the Immortality Ode in particular. He effects this reconciliation by calling the passages to which he objects "bad philosophy," while enjoying separately the overall feeling the poem gives him:

> At the conclusion of the Poems came the famous Ode, falsely called Platonic, "Intimations of Immortality": in which, along with more than his usual sweetness of melody and rhythm, and along with the two passages of grand imagery but bad philosophy so often quoted, I found that he too had had similar experience to mine; that he also had felt that the first freshness of youthful enjoyment of life was not lasting; but that he had sought for compensation, and found it, in the way in which he was now teaching me to find it. The result was that I gradually, but completely, emerged from my habitual depression and was never again subject to it. (89-90)

Poetry becomes for him effectively divorced from belief and philosophy, and Mill is able to stomach the sweet medicine of Wordsworth's poem without vomiting up the positivism that brought on his disease. It is only a small step further for us to accept that the poem and its philosophy were distinct for the poet as well; and by taking that step, we gain the self-assurance and security that comes with never having to confront *foreign* ideas in poetry as *serious* ideas.

Variations on Mill's approach seem to have worked for some later critics; as we saw in chapter 5, John Mathison was able to reconcile the "nonsense" of pre-existence with his appreciation of the Ode by discarding the "unnecessary" hypothesis after using it as a bridge to "understanding"

(439). Others, such as M. H. Abrams, have found this more difficult: although he grants Wordsworth "his initial predication, or myth, or *donnée*," Abrams decides that a poet "must still win our imaginative consent" and cannot "evade his responsibility to the beliefs and prepossessions of our common experience" (133-34). Richard Hoffpauir goes so far as to say that the Ode loses even emotional appeal on account of its "idealistic philosophy": the Immortality Ode fails to move us as would a poem on death, for example, "because death is a fact and rebirth only a hope and pre-existence only a theory" (82). These kinds of objections have necessitated more arcane methods of reconciling the Ode to positivism.

In chapter 5, we saw how some critics tried to read the Immortality Ode allegorically to make it accord with mainstream Christianity, while others diverted our attention to the issue of Wordsworth's sincere belief in God. Similar strategies appear in readings by positivist critics such as Leslie Stephen and Edward Proffitt, who try to turn Wordsworth into a prophet of Darwinism, and Lionel Trilling, who emphasizes Wordsworth's orthodox naturalism. Like the early Christian mythographers, these critics engage in the subtle process of making the great art of a former age accord with the orthodoxies of the present and, through this alchemy, safe for consumption. Although Stephen, Proffitt, and Trilling are not representative of all twentieth-century criticism (some of which manifestly rejects positivism) I feel that they nonetheless evince biases that are merely less obvious in others.

Leslie Stephen, writing in the 1870s, illustrates the confluence of religious and positivistic prejudices in his dismissal of pre-existence: for him, there was no question "whether it is reasonable or orthodox to believe that 'our birth is but a sleep and a forgetting'" (2.259). He makes it his concern, however, to show that the Immortality Ode may yet prove reconcilable with science, which he accomplishes by translating Wordsworth's "celestial light" into "the glory and freshness of our childish instincts":

Some modern reasoners would explain [the glory]'s significance by reference to a very different kind of pre-existence. The instincts, they would say, are valuable, because they register the accumulated and inherited experiences of past generations. Wordsworth's delight in wild scenery is regarded by them as due to the "combination of states that were organised in the race during barbarous times, when its pleasurable activities were amongst the mountains, woods, and waters." In childhood we are most completely under the dominion of these inherited impulses.[2]

Stephen subsequently intuits that Wordsworth would have repudiated these ideas "with disgust," but he seems much less concerned with respecting Wordsworth's intentions than with making the poet speak for contemporary science. Such an appropriation might be warranted were the ideas of the poem left intact, treated comprehensively, and placed in the context of Wordsworth's other works; Stephen, however, equates "celestial light" (Ode 4) with a positivist notion of "childish instincts" (2.259) without considering the possibility that Wordsworth *really means* celestial light when he says "celestial light," and that the "High instincts" of line 147 may refer to something altogether different from a "barbarous" instinct. Furthermore, Stephen fails to notice—as so many critics have—that the poet briefly regains his ability to see this light in "Composed upon an Evening of extraordinary Splendour and Beauty," which should preclude us from reading the light as a metaphor for childish instincts. By ignoring these issues, Stephen diverts our attention away from the heterodox idea of spiritual pre-existence and into the world of biological pre-existence.

A similar strategy is employed by Edward Proffitt, who wishes to see in Wordsworth's sea-shore figure in stanza 9 of the Ode the anticipation of Darwin's theory of evolution. Proffitt, apparently intent on rehabilitating Wordsworth in the name of positivism, contradicts the rest of the Ode (and Wordsworth's *oeuvre*) and defies the most obvious conventions of metaphoric explication to effect his reading:

I suggest that in the lines in question from the Ode [161-68], Wordsworth brings into harmony his characteristic developmental view of human growth and a developmental (i.e., evolutionary) conception of the human habitat. That is, having struggled with his own urge toward transcendence, Wordsworth comes to see that our true "home" is not "God" (l.65) but earth, with its natural history.... It is the sea that is called "immortal," and it is now from the sea, rather than from heaven, that we are said to have come. We did not, then, spring into being by an act of special creation, but are creatures of a natural developmental process, the record of which lies in the landscape. (89)

Amazingly, we find Proffitt quoting part of the very lines he openly contradicts: "we come / From God, who is our home" (64-65), a move to which he appears to foresee no objections. Of course, Wordsworth nowhere suggests that we evolved from sea creatures, and Proffitt's discovery that Wordsworth was interested in geology, coupled with his misreading of the sea metaphor in stanza 9, cannot alter this. Yet this does not deter Proffitt from going further to suggest that "the title of the Ode is possibly misleading" because he finds the poem "veers away from intimations of immortality as such to focus solely on mortality" (90). That such presumptuous exegesis can appear in a scholarly journal—*The Wordsworth Circle*, 1982—seems to me possible only in a milieu where positivistic orthodoxy is such that the most specious connection to Darwin, the positivist saviour, is considered grounds for a serious argument.

I feel I must apologize for discussing Lionel Trilling in a group with Proffitt and Stephen, for I find Trilling's reading of the Ode extremely restrained and lucid. But he, too, tries to make Wordsworth speak for positivism while questioning whether the Immortality Ode is about immortality and pre-existence.

Trilling is too good a critic to contradict Wordsworth openly, but he does translate Wordsworth's poem into a scientific vocabulary acceptable to positivist orthodoxy. This is mainly a matter of Trilling's reformulating the "vision splendid," the "celestial light," and the "visionary gleam" as parts of an "optical phenomenon" (132). For Trilling, Wordsworth's loss of vision becomes an "'optical' change in himself," and by the end of the poem "[w]e are back again at optics, which we have never really left..." (133; 152). Since optics is the science of light, and the poem is at least partially about lost light, such a reformulation is not entirely unwarranted. But the study of perception is considered separately from optics *per se*; when a person claims to perceive the world differently than he did heretofore, science does not look for an explanation in optics, which is a branch of physics, but in ophthalmology or psychology. What Trilling tries to achieve by placing "celestial light" in the purview of optics, then, is a reformulation of Wordsworth's experience in terms that sound like hard science.

The rhetorical positivism of Trilling's terminology becomes more evident when we discover that he fully realizes Wordsworth is not talking about ordinary light:

> Celestial light probably means only something different from ordinary, earthly, scientific light; it is a light of the mind, shining even in darkness.... (132)

Trilling almost seems to be unaware of the inaccuracy of referring to this light as an "optical phenomenon," but his choice of terminology accords with his explicit intention of being "as naturalistic as possible in speaking of Wordsworth's childhood experiences and the more-or-less Platonic notion they suggested to him" (147). By speaking of "something different from ordinary, earthly, scientific light" as though it were a matter of optics, Trilling translates the theological language of the Ode to make it speak for his naturalistic imperative.

Although I agree that the Ode is a record of experience and in this way is "naturalistic in its intention," I think it would be wrong to say that it is so "despite its dominating theistical metaphor" (Trilling 149); Wordsworth's naturalistic observations are intimately connected with the claims he makes in stanza 5, for example, in that they (the claims) offer to explain these observations. But Trilling tries to erase this connection by emphasizing Wordsworth's naturalism, thus making of Wordsworth a positivist prophet and recreating him in the image of a modern naturalist.

Trilling's strategy is carried further in his attempt to connect Wordsworth and psychoanalysis—a dubious science, but a science nonetheless in Trilling's eyes:

> The naturalistic tone of the Wordsworth [Fenwick] note suggests that we shall be doing no violence to the experience of the "vanishings" if we consider it scientifically. In a well-known essay, "Stages in the Development of the Sense of Reality," the distinguished psychoanalyst Ferenczi speaks of the child's reluctance to distinguish between himself and the world and of the slow growth of objectivity which differentiates the self from external things. (144)

What Trilling is doing is quite similar to what I have tried to do in chapter 3, namely connect Wordsworth's testimony with the latest research in psychology. Trilling differs, however, in that he goes about this at the expense of the notion of pre-existence, which he feels justified in ignoring after bringing up Wordsworth's apparent repudiation of it in the Fenwick note. Like David Rogers—who, as we saw in chapter 5, elides pre-existence by pointing out Wordsworth's references to Enoch, Elijah, and other signs of religious orthodoxy—Trilling ignores pre-existence by pointing to the parts of the Fenwick note that accord with his naturalistic imperative: the parts where Wordsworth describes his childhood perceptions. This approach ultimately enables Trilling to imply that the Ode might not even be about immortality at all:

The knowledge of man's mortality—this must be carefully noted in a poem *presumably* about immortality—now replaces the "glory" as the agency which makes things significant and precious. (152; emphasis mine)

Since it remains connected to the "dominating theistical metaphor" that naturalism supposedly nullifies, immortality's significance to the poem dwindles in proportion to Trilling's emphasis on Wordsworth's naturalism. Thus, with Trilling's help, the poem begins to accord with a positivistic faith that does not look through death; it begins to become universally relevant and justifiably anthologized because it replaces "glory" with the "knowledge of man's mortality" accessible to us all.

As I hope to have made clear, the strategies of Trilling, Proffitt, Stephen, and other critics who have tried to make Wordsworth speak for positivism blend into the strategies of those who have made him speak for orthodox religion, just as the heresy-seekers among the religious are supplemented by the positivist heresy-seekers. Hence, criticism continues to prevent the Immortality Ode from announcing a belief in pre-existence to new readers who would rather see more conventional ideas in the poem. This does not end with the positivist critics. In the next chapter, we shall discover how the newest of these new readers have approached the Ode with a new set of orthodoxies, but how these retain the old structures of ventriloquism and inquisition at the expense of the perennial heresy of pre-existence.

Chapter 7

The Immortality Ode vs. Postmodern Orthodoxies

We have seen how some critics have tried to elide or transmute the claim of disembodied consciousness in the Immortality Ode to make the poem accord with the positivist assumption that any claim to disembodied consciousness is a pernicious lie. For what I shall call *postmodern orthodoxy*, this basic assumption remains. What seems to have changed, however, are the reasons why a claim to disembodied consciousness cannot be entertained: whereas the positivist readers find in it an obstruction of both knowledge and humanistic politics, the postmoderns see in such a claim the repression of material concerns, whether materialist politics, "the body" and its desires, or material signifiers, that is, written words. This shift in reasons seems to have added to the difficulty of reconciling Wordsworth's Ode to the new orthodoxies, for the rebellion of the new guard against the techniques of the old makes contemporary critics more inclined to expose Wordsworth's heresy than to elide it.

In chapter 2, I argued the absurdity of Marjorie Levinson's interpretation of the Ode's "visionary gleam" as "the worldly renewal heralded by the French Revolution" (102); Wordsworth makes it clear in a poem of 1817 that the same gleam he thought "forever taken from [his] sight" (Ode 177) had since been briefly restored on an evening of extraordinary splendour and beauty. In chapter 4, I noted the possibility of reading "a Tree, of many, one" as the "single tree" of *The Prelude* (6.90), a reading far less problematic than Levinson's "Tree of Liberty" identification (109). I did not speculate, however, about the reasons why Levinson is so eager to discover political significations.

If it is not already apparent, it is clear from her conclusions that Levinson is motivated by an inquisitorial desire to expose Wordsworth's deviation from Revolutionary orthodoxy. She finds that by the end of the poem, Wordsworth has turned to the pursuit of "victories... far greater than those once anticipated from the French revolution" (114), namely spiritual victories that Levinson aligns with his putative loss of interest in material history. It would be difficult to argue that Wordsworth did not deviate thus—Book 11 of *The Prelude* tells the story of his early enthusiasm for and later disillusionment with the Revolution—but to suggest that the Ode is a political allegory about his loss of faith in revolution necessitates an elision of too much evidence to the contrary, and in particular of *every* recorded statement Wordsworth made about the poem afterwards.[1] Yet Levinson cannot stop herself from seeing political significance in details, such as the "imperial palace" of line 85, that even she can see do not accord with her reading:

> In characterizing mankind's native dimension (its being's heart and home) as an imperial palace, Wordsworth not only appoints the protective enclosure over imaginative expansion (so-called Romantic Nature), he adopts the language of the Royalist position.

> Although he undercuts the elitism of the phrase by representing this mansion as a universal source, universally inaccessible, the allusion identifies Wordsworth's vision as a critique of the Revolution's millenial thrust. Likewise the epithet "Nature's priest" at once inscribes and negates the Revolutionary program. (112)

Levinson makes it sound as though "the allusion identifies," whereas she has both conjured the supposed allusion and made the identification: a repression of her agency that to me suggests unacknowledged politics in *her* writing. Although she begins her essay talking about the French Revolution, one senses that Levinson is talking about all Revolution, and that Wordsworth is being castigated for failing to provide future Marxists with a cultural foothold in his poetry. But if Levinson is not inquisitorially exhibiting the images of transcendental existence (the palace and the priest) on behalf of Marxism, she is at least uncovering them with Marxist hermeneutics on behalf of the Enlightenment Revolutionary program: the "imperial palace," however universally inaccessible, *must* be a symbol of elitism (even though Levinson concedes this elitism is "undercut"), and any epithet with "priest" in it *must* negate Revolutions, no matter how metaphorically it is employed (religion being the "opiate of the masses").

As for pre-existence, it must, as a myth, belong to ideology and is therefore always to be deprecated, whether the poet takes it seriously or not; and to Levinson, Wordsworth is all the more culpable (and pitiful) for resorting to myth instead of the explicit ideology:

> In sum, Wordsworth's myth of the soul, a pragmatic narrative never assimilated into his thinking, situates his grief over the failure of the Revolution and the invalidation of its ideology within a vision so vast and impersonal as to 'disappear' that pain. (113-14)

I think we can translate this passage thus: "in sum, Levinson's myth of Wordsworth's ideology, a materialist narrative never assimilated to the poem, situates her grief over the failure of Marxism and the invalidation of its ideology within a vision so vast and impersonal as to 'disappear' that pain." If this translation seems overspeculative and unfair to Levinson, I think the same verdict should be applied to her translation of Wordsworth.

Levinson's reading resembles those of the religious-allegorical critics in allegorizing pre-existence as something related to her own worldview, namely a political default. Unlike the earlier critics, however, she executes this procedure to facilitate a critique instead of an assimilation.

As I have remarked, it becomes conveniently irrelevant to a reading like Levinson's whether Wordsworth believed in pre-existence or not. Yet we should question whether the assumption that Wordsworth did not believe in it somehow prompts a reading that *makes* the issue irrelevant: in other words, if we posited that Wordsworth fully believed that "Our birth is but a sleep and a forgetting," would critics be as quick to presume that the statement signifies something else? It seems to me that the possibility of Wordsworth's belief might even give as ideologically-oriented a critic as Levinson some pause in her hermeneutic project.

Jeffrey C. Robinson and Gene Ruoff are also interested in subjecting Wordsworth to postmodern orthodoxies, although their readings require less forceful hermeneutics than Levinson's. Robinson's strategy involves rather a genealogical approach: tracing a few phrases of the Ode back to an earlier poem, "The Mad Monk," he concludes that the Ode must have been about the same experience that produced the earlier poem—that is, before Wordsworth repressed and sublimated this original experience beyond recognition. Robinson decides that the reference to pre-existence is part of this sublimation, whereby bodily desires are supplanted (or sup-plemented) by a desire for something transcendent ("God, who is our home"). Ruoff argues for a similar process of sublimation, but claims a special role for pre-existence *per se*: the doctrine, Ruoff argues, implies a spirit-body duality strongly privileging the spirit. Hence, pre-existence is as heretical a doctrine for the postmodern body-cult[2] as it was for the Synod of Constantinople, which excommunicated Origen for believing it.

William Hazlitt, a contemporary of Wordsworth's, becomes the ultimate authority on the Immortality Ode for Jeffrey Robinson. Quoting from Hazlitt's essay "Romeo and Juliet," Robinson discovers him averring that the "glory" of the Ode was really "the passion of love" and the "delight of novelty."[3] Robinson briefly considers that Hazlitt "perhaps has no right to conflate infancy with youth" but then drops all reservations:

> [Hazlitt] may have a point when he suggests that Wordsworth had misdefined the origins of the splendour and glory in our first impressions of things. As Trilling says: "despite its dominating theistic metaphor, the Ode is largely naturalistic in intention." More precisely, the poet has substituted a false for a true origin, a "celestial" for a passional and completely human one. Hazlitt, brilliantly anticipating Wordsworth's late disclaimer that the theological construct of our origins had been nothing more than a metaphor, comes close to saying that the complicated experience of passion is Wordsworth's real subject against which he has defended himself with theology. ("The Immortality Ode" 65)

Robinson agrees with Trilling's claim about the Ode's "naturalism," accepts Hazlitt's assumption that Wordsworth substituted a false for a true origin, and then assumes that Wordsworth's "late disclaimer" irrevocably turns "the theological construct" into "nothing more than a metaphor," even though the Fenwick note is manifestly palliative and therefore suspect. This last move is particularly unjustified based on Robinson's own premise, namely that Wordsworth "defended himself with theology" against his "real subject": to Robinson, it seems, pre-existence and orthodox theology are of a piece, and it does not occur to him that Wordsworth might "defend himself" with orthodox theology against the original, heterodox subject of pre-existence.

Robinson tries to support his argument by adducing the evidence of Wordsworth's "The Mad Monk" (c. 1800), a poem about the "sexual pleasures" Robinson decides are sublimated in the Ode. As he remarks, stanza 2 of "The Mad Monk" is very similar to the Ode's first stanza:

> There was a time when earth, and sea, and skies,
>   The bright green vale and forest's dark recess,
> When all things lay before my eyes
>   In steady loveliness.
> But now I feel on earth's uneasy scene
>   Such motions as will never cease!
>   I only ask for peace—
> Then wherefore must I know, that such a time has been![4]

As Robinson explains, the lines are sung by a mad monk "who has killed his beloved out of jealousy" (66). Because of the similarity of this opening to the Ode, he suggests that "the shock or rift of madness and murder, the connection between sexual passion and active destruction…lies buried at the core of the apparently seamless Ode" (66). The obvious objection to such a claim—"that Wordsworth simply applied the rhetorical and rhythmical scaffolding of this ["Mad Monk"] stanza to the Ode" (66)—Robinson acknowledges; but he proposes to overcome this gaping hole in his theory by suggesting that such a reapplication of the "scaffolding" is "unlikely" (66). Why it should be unlikely, he does not say. It seems it is unlikely only because it does not accord with his program of turning the Ode into a sordid, sublimated tale of sex and violence.

In *Radical Literary Education*, Robinson develops his argument further, treating "The Mad Monk" as an early draft of the Immortality Ode. He calls it a "noteworthy revision" when "the loss of the gleam is not occasioned by an event" in the Ode, whereas the loss of the "steady loveliness" in the earlier poem "belongs to history and biography" (126). It never occurs to Robinson that "steady loveliness" and "visionary gleam" might not refer to the same thing, in which case the different circumstances of their loss cannot be a "revision." That they do not refer to the same thing is not only deducible from the radically different contexts in which these phrases appear, but also by the fact that for the Ode's speaker, "lovely is the Rose" (11)—"steady loveliness" is still present to him, but he cannot see the "visionary gleam."

Robinson tries to solidify his argument by examining Wordsworth's revisions to the Ode from the manuscript drafts of 1802-4 to the unpublished manuscripts of 1849-50. What he claims to discover is "an unmistakable trend toward the elimination of almost all references to the senses, passion, and even fantasy" (*Radical* 115)—implying, of course, that Wordsworth represses the sex and violence of "The Mad Monk" further as he gets older. Robinson's best example of this process is the revision of lines 122-23, which in 1815 read "Thou little child, yet glorious in the might / Of heaven-born freedom on thy being's height," changed from "might / Of untam'd pleasures, on thy Being's height" in 1807. I must concede Robinson's point here; the earlier lines imply a much more visceral experience ("untam'd pleasures"); but given the context of the "eternal mind," and "Immortality," which appear in the same stanza, I think the visceral is meant to represent the spiritual in this case. "Untam'd" remains an apt characterization of spiritual pleasures that precede socialization. But since Robinson is intent on eliminating almost all references to the spiritual, he returns us to a positivist allegory:

> The phrase, "might / Of untam'd pleasures," is at once cast down the long avenue of the classical tradition of the precarious but necessary balance between our "lower" and "higher" selves while it looks forward to the revolutionary Darwinian and Freudian intimacies with our "animal" nature. Wordsworth seems here to admit to the power, or might, of drives and instinct and pleasure itself and their determining place in the process of growing up. (*Radical* 114)

Once again, Wordsworth is turned into a prophet for science. But Robinson is no mere positivist critic, and he shows how Wordsworth is also a culpably reluctant prophet of postmodern hedonism: the poet "seems here to admit to the power" of "pleasure itself," but represses this in subsequent revisions.

In his zeal to show Wordsworth's repressions, Robinson goes so far as to suppress parts of the very manuscript evidence he introduces. For example, he takes "the most revealing revision" to be the omission of manuscript material at line 155:

> ... a master light of all our seeing;
> Thrown off from us or mitigate our spell
> Of that strong frame of sense in which we dwell
> Uphold us,...

Noticing the "strong frame of sense in which we dwell," Robinson claims that "this line states emphatically that the body defines us and organizes our relationship to the world" (*Radical* 117). What he suppresses is that the "strong frame of sense" is introduced as "our spell": the body is the stuff of illusion, merely transitory like a cold spell. This elision of Robinson's is further compounded by his selection of manuscript, which in this case is the Commonplace Book.[5] In this version, the lines are hampered by the fact that "thrown" becomes an attribute of "master light" instead of a verb we expect to be parallel to "mitigate" and "uphold"; Wordsworth thus appears to say that the "master light" is "[t]hrown off from us," which supports readings of the light as common imaginative light. If we look at the more legible Longman manuscript, however, we see that the lines read "[t]hrow off from us, or mitigate, the spell / Of that strong frame of sense..." (qtd. in *PW* 4.283). In this version, "throw" is properly parallel to "mitigate," and it is thus clearer that the body is a "spell" that the "master light" can throw off or mitigate—an ability that for Wordsworth "doth breed / Perpetual benediction" (Ode 134-35).

What is particularly disturbing about Robinson's biased hermeneutics is that he manages, as he tells us in *Radical Literary Education*, to convince many of his students that his way of approaching the poem is correct. Of course, he makes it sound as though his students have arrived at the same conclusions as he has by *anamnesis* induced by dialectic. He calls it his "biggest discovery" that "the adolescents studying Wordsworth with me found so compelling Hazlitt's criticism that the 'Ode' has substituted childhood (as idyll) for its real subject, adolescence" (164). I think it is painfully obvious that the reason they found Hazlitt "compelling" is that Robinson found him so. What is worse, Robinson seems to be proud that he has liberated his repressed students in the process:

> [F]inally they could, with Hazlitt as advocate, withdraw from the regressed identification with the child as the container of happiness and recover their more libidinal and aggressive adolescent selves. (164)

One wonders if it is not the professor who is trying to recover or suppress something. Could it be that he, unconsciously, wants to withdraw from the identification with adulthood as "the container of happiness" and recover his own more "libidinous and aggressive adolescent" self?

As I have remarked, Robinson's exegesis subsumes the issue of pre-existence in a body-spirit dualism where pre-existence becomes functionally equivalent to any spiritual doctrine: pre-existence merely signifies sublimation of carnal desires, a sublimation that a number of other theological constructs, orthodox or otherwise, could have facilitated. A similar conclusion is reached by Gene Ruoff in his 1989 study, *Wordsworth and Coleridge: The Making of the Major Lyrics 1802-1804*. Ruoff, however, is suspicious of "critics" who "turn the [first four stanza of the Ode] into a version of 'The Mad Monk'," even though he finds "[t]he Ode's echo of this absurdly trite poem unsettling" (57; 53). Ruoff extracts repressed carnality in more subtle ways: first, he suggests that by energizing "the conventions of erotic pastoral, [the Ode] throws itself open to a vast array of its tawdry progeny of the late eighteenth century" (53), implying that this "erotic pastoral" is suppressed in Wordsworth. Second, and more significant, is Ruoff's discovery that the notion of pre-existence may be connected to the early Christian heretic Origen: since Origenist pre-existence "is inevitably hostile to the flesh," Wordsworth's pre-existence betokens a similar asceticism that is only partially counterbalanced by the glimmerings of orthodoxy and humanism in the Ode. As Ruoff puts it, "Wordsworth rescues the despised flesh from its Origenist entrapment… largely through a secularized version of the fortunate fall, a paradox with which he was well acquainted" (267).

Ruoff provides very little evidence that Wordsworth's doctrine is specifically Origenist. He assumes that Wordsworth's version of pre-existence is "the most Westernized, most Christianized form of the doctrine" since it appears to limit the soul's journey to a single cycle of fall, birth, and ascent; and from this assumption he facilely deduces that "[t]he myth Wordsworth presents was first articulated by Origen," (253). Of course, there is no indication in the Ode that Wordsworth rules out reincarnation, and his figure of "[t]he Soul that rises with us, our life's Star" carries the possibility of diurnal repetition. But Ruoff is determined to link Wordsworth to the most ascetic exponent of pre-existence he can find in order to expose the poet's heresy against the orthodox postmodern body-cult:

> My purpose…has not been to suggest that because the early church had discredited pre-existence, Wordsworth could not have credited it. I have wanted to bring forward tensions in the doctrine's initial formulation which we have already seen at work in Wordsworth's Ode. The belief is inevitably hostile to the flesh, the senses, and to the material creation. It engenders a religion of withdrawal, asceticism, and contemplation, severely limited in its

ability to value human life lived in time. The doctrine of pre-existence is the product of a hunger for absolutes that threatens always
to extinguish the present. If we push Origen's system one step further, the entire history of humankind, including the advent of
Christ, becomes little more than a stain on the white radiance of
eternity. (255-56)

Here, Ruoff not only implies just how repressive Wordsworth was in
even dissembling belief in pre-existence, but also gives us a sermon about
the belief's persistently pernicious and heretical character. Like a modern-
day Justinian, Ruoff makes it his object to excommunicate Origen all over
again, only this time on the grounds of Origen's asceticism, which does
not accord with postmodern hedonism, and Origen's "hunger for
absolutes," which does not accord with postmodern relativism and privileging of "the present." And like many early theologians, who "contested
each other's orthodoxy (and good repute) by hurling charges of
'Origenism' at their opponents" (Clark 3), Ruoff constructs Origen's
Christianity as something radically different from orthodox Christianity.
Ruoff implies that Origen's self-castration was precipitated by his belief in
pre-existence (255), whereas Ruoff's source, Johannes Quasten, tells us
that Origen did this because he took "Matthew 19,12 in too literal a
sense" (2.38); and Origen's lifelong asceticism seems to have been determined more by his desire to imitate Christ than his belief in pre-existence
(Quasten 2.96). Furthermore, regardless of what Origen believed, we have
no reason to assume that pre-existence is "inevitably hostile to the flesh";
one's preference for a disembodied state need indicate no more hostility to
incarnation than a preference for leisure implies a hostility towards work,
even if one's ultimate goal is a state of permanent leisure.

Once again, we find that the issue of pre-existence in the Immortality
Ode comes down to a dispute over doctrine, much as we found it in
Coleridge. As Ruoff himself acknowledges on the history of pre-existence
in general, "because both the appeals of the doctrine and its consequences

are curiously static, entering into the discourse at one cultural moment is very much like entering at any other" (252). I think we have progressed somewhat, however, when we find the dispute brought into the open by Ruoff, even though his tractate against pre-existence appears in the guise of a digression. We can at least see from his assumptions and representations that prejudice vitiates his reading, and we can therefore compensate for whatever biases this prejudice introduces.

In *The Unremarkable Wordsworth*, Geoffrey Hartman declines the inquisitorial urge in the approaches of Ruoff and Robinson. For Hartman, the Ode is a text that can be made to speak like and for poststructuralism, just as Wordsworth is for him a prophet of Heidegger; in fact, he makes this ventriloquistic project explicit when he claims to "turn to Wordsworth because to 'translate' Heidegger we must choose a text at home in the English literary tradition" (202). Hartman notes that both Wordsworth and Heidegger refer to *anamnesis* "in relation to our forgetfulness of Being," which gives him the cue to extract the postmodern doctrine of the supremacy of indeterminate reference from Wordsworth's Ode.

Having taxed myself with interpreting Wordsworth's poetry, I would be loth to deny the unstable signification that pervades it. But Hartman seems intent on making this instability appear more pronounced than it is, and he illustrates it by referring to Wordsworth's panegyric on the "best Philosopher"—a passage no more "stable" in its meaning than any other, I suppose, which leads me to wonder why Hartman has singled it out. For Hartman, however, stanza 8 is not merely an example of indeterminate reference; it is the *quintessence* of indeterminate reference, a *"discours de la folie"* in which "nonsense is uttered" (203). Hartman seems predisposed to discover nonsense, however, and he seems determined to convince us of his discovery by providing a nonsensical reading of lines 111-13, "Thou Eye among the blind / That, deaf and silent, read'st the eternal deep,…" etc.:

This eye may be the moon, should a cosmic representation be involved.Or, God's eye in the position of the moon; and the problem of reference or attribution (of finding a subject to which these properties may be ascribed) perplexes the reader who must decide what "deaf and silent" refer to, and whether it is the child that is haunted by the eternal mind, or whether it is the eternal deep, read by the child, that is so haunted. What a night-piece! The Abyss itself is put *en abîme*. (205)

Hartman concludes that "Wordsworth's language seems to corrode stable reference" (205); yet Hartman seems unwilling to search for "stable reference," which, in the case of this passage, would necessitate our discovering why Wordsworth speaks of the child as an "Eye among the blind." Apparently determined to discover the fashionable "problem of reference or attribution" in the poem, Hartman provides a reading that makes this problem appear more pronounced than it is; unable to find a "subject" in the passage, "in the sense of ego" (205), Hartman concludes that Wordsworth anticipates Heidegger: "the subject evaporates, like the word 'Being' in Heidegger's view..." (206).

Hartman's ingenuity in these hermeneutics reaches its apex when he begins to wonder about the possibility that Wordsworth represses linguistic signification in the Ode:

There are more insidious questions about reading: why is hearing elided into the image of a "deaf and silent" reading? Does the sound *ear* break through nevertheless in "exterior" (108) and "Seer" (114)? Even the word "read'st" seems to contain that (scrambled) ear. (205)

In his effort to expose Wordsworth's repressed exemplification of hearing privileged over writing, Hartman ultimately turns to the anagrammatic method, finding "ear" scrambled in "read'st." His *rea*ding thus becomes like the work of Jonathan Swift's "Tribnian" exegetes, who when unable to discover treasons through symbolic misreadings of correspondence, rearrange the letters to prove their targets guilty.[6]

As for the doctrine of pre-existence, it suits Hartman perfectly that Wordsworth claims to use it as an Archimedean lever with which to move "the world of his own mind" (*PW* 4.464):

> Under the pressure of finding this strange Archimedean lever, this "point whereon to rest"—the subject evaporates, like the word "Being" in Heidegger's view, and what remains is the self-generating strength of a hyperbolic language movement, a *Thou* that echoes an equally ecstatic *Now*. (206)

By accepting Wordsworth's denial of serious belief in pre-existence, Hartman quite correctly identifies in Wordsworth's "lever" an absent referent; a speaker tells us "Our sleep is but a birth and a forgetting," but the subject, the believer of this statement is nowhere to be found. Hence, Hartman's acceptance of this denial becomes a point upon which his argument rests, and he is thus always already prevented from questioning this point.

A similar reliance on Wordsworth's lever analogy obtains in a reading by Fred Hoerner, who goes further than Hartman in rehabilitating Wordsworth for postmodern orthodoxy. Hoerner argues that Wordsworth enacts the "practice theories" of Pierre Bordieu and Anthony Giddens in the Immortality Ode when the poet gains agency within structural constraints:

> Wordsworth aims to use mental custom against itself, a goal he images in the Fenwick note as an Archimedean fulcrum point "whereon to rest his machine"; once gained, that point empowers the poet to leverage off the weight of "his own mind." I suggest that killing weight leveraged breeds joy because the poet has

gained agency from the customary formalism that is nostalgia's inertial freight. (631)

Hoerner supplies us with a wonderfully apt figure for this application of practice theory to the poem. He tells us it is his desire "to wed the *Ode* to theory in ways that let theory gain from Wordsworth" (632). This wedding therefore brings a dowry to theory, and one suspects that this is an arranged marriage in which the poem-bride will be forced to do things against her will.

Hoerner's argument focuses on the transition between stanzas 8 and 9, that is, on the sudden expression of joy after the Ode's nadir. He reads this joy as arising from a sense of agency, figured through the "embers" of stanza 9, regained within the containing structure of a binary, either-or thinking which has offered only the "static" images of the seer-child and the imitative child in stanza 8:

> [I]f the child eludes one "Master," the haunting presence of immortality, he takes on the burden of another: the earthly body, custom, "palsied age" and death. Thus, the narration concludes on a note of double-loss, a double-bind because either position denies life by sealing it up in oppressive stasis…. The life that subsequently springs from the "embers" at the opening of stanza 9 figures an awakened sense of agency and accident rekindled through structure. (642)

Hoerner's reading thus necessitates that we read the "seer blest" and his condition as something Wordsworth breaks away from rather than yearns toward, a reading which relies heavily on the ominous suggestions of the master-slave figure of line 120. As I noted in chapter 4, this is facilitated by the critics' not allowing that the perinatal state of a seer-child might be blissful, as Traherne tells us and as Wordsworth states: "Heaven lies about us in our infancy" (66). According to Hoerner, Wordsworth's joy is not a matter of recalling this bliss; it is a matter of "[t]urning from the celestial" (643). But the poet suggests that he will "find / Strength in what remains behind" of the celestial "radiance which was once so bright" (Ode 181; 176). Like Trilling, Hoerner concludes that the poem is not about "Intimations of Immortality" after all: for him, Wordsworth relinquishes "the 'one delight' of symbolic immediacy and immortality" for the postmodern consolation of "identity as a narrative that time will undercut" (649).

Like other critics whom we have observed making Wordsworth speak for their philosophy, Hoerner must extract peculiar significations from the Ode's imagery while ignoring passages that problematize these extractions. This is exemplified by his exegesis of the embers figure that begins stanza 9:

> If we hold on to the figure's materiality, two qualities make "embers" evocative of the dialectical turn Wordsworth makes in stanza 9. First of all, embers "live"—catch fire—only if they are acted on, when fanned, blown, or broken. Second, they live by consuming their container; the fire bursts out from but only by means [sic] of the remains that hold it in place.... That the container also fuels life speaks concisely for Wordsworth's disfiguration of the ideology implicit in the Romantic symbol. (642-43)

Returning to the poem, we find no evidence that the "embers" burst into flame, consume their container, or even that they *could* do these things. Furthermore, if we respect the imagistic grammar of the poem, in which light is the dominant figure starting from line four's "celestial light," we inevitably read the embers as mere dwindled light; their "materiality," as Hoerner puts it, only becomes relevant when we force them to speak for materialism.

Hoerner also makes much of Wordsworth's reflection at the end of the Ode, when the poet tells the "Fountains, Meadows, Hills, and Groves" that he has only "relinquished one delight / To live beneath [their] more habitual sway" (188-92). Hoerner dissects the lines and removes the words "habitual" which he facilely equates with Bordieu's *habitus*, and "sway," which he equates with the play of *différance*:

> "Habitual" highlights the structured sense of the habitus, yet also evokes the fitting sense of a pattern without an absolute center as opposed to the essentialism of natural law. "Sway" further decenters the phrase through its etymological friction between "swing" and "rule, dominion." If we take Wordsworth's lead and wedge critical thought between meanings, "habitual sway" characterizes the dialectic that animates convention late in the Ode. (649-50)

Hoerner's ingenuity here is quite admirable, but he still fails to account for the context of the lines. Since Wordsworth tells the natural world "I feel your might" in line 190, we are bound to read "sway" in 192 as the dominance of that "might." We are so bound, that is, unless it is our imperative to make the poem speak against any kind of dominance, bondage, ideology, and exclusive significations. Since this can be accomplished only when a critic dominates the text with his theory, such imperatives undercut themselves; and I find Hoerner, as such a critic, thoroughly hypocritical when he suggests that his reading will be accepted "provided that readers resist their desire to master the text" (650). Hoerner tries to master the text as much as anyone, which I would not find particularly culpable in itself—*mea culpa*—but one should be able to admit to this "desire."

The marriage of theory and the Immortality Ode is successful in that it "let[s] theory gain from Wordsworth," as Hoerner planned; but I find that the Ode has gained nothing from theory, and the bride has been forced to give up her religion to please the groom and his family. Hoerner accepts that Wordsworth treated the notion of pre-existence "rather pragmatically" (634) and concludes that the poet treated structural constraints in the same way. Hence, the issue of pre-existence is elided as conveniently and as necessarily as it was in *Biographia Literaria*: I say *necessarily* elided, for to posit that Wordsworth took pre-existence seriously is to abrogate the absence of signification upon which readings such as Hoerner's stand.

I hope to have illustrated in this chapter the remarkable persistence of not only prejudice against the idea of pre-existence and its importance in Wordsworth, but also the perennial strategies by which pre-existence in the Ode is ignored or translated into something entirely different to suit a current orthodoxy. It was not my intent to call into question the relevance of postmodern reading techniques for Wordsworth in general, for I think these techniques may yet prove valuable in approaching the Immortality Ode if critics consider the possibility of Wordsworth's belief in pre-existence, and if they become more aware of what such belief may entail.

Afterword

In both my interpretation of the Immortality Ode and my evaluation of other critics' interpretations, I believe I have demonstrated the value of approaching the Immortality Ode as though Wordsworth believed in pre-existence, and as though such a belief were more than just a fantastic, foreign superstition. I have discovered within the Ode consistencies of thought and imagery heretofore unremarked in commentary, and have shown how these also accord with Wordsworth's other writings. That I needed to doubt Wordsworth's late apology to facilitate this reading seems to me justified by the questionable motives behind the apology.

Whatever perspicacity I have achieved in this inquiry, and whatever success I have achieved in recommending the fruitfulness of my approach, should be at least partially attributed to the extent to which my serious consideration of pre-existence coincides with Wordsworth's, insofar as his ideas are legible to us and freed from the dominance of the Fenwick note apology. Just as a Christian brings an elucidative sympathy to a work like *Paradise Lost* and thus benefits even non-Christian readers, I hope to have brought an elucidative sympathy to Wordsworth that should benefit readers who will not or cannot believe in a prior state of existence. If my sympathy has shaded into enthusiasm at times, I hope the reader will recognize the inevitability of such transgressions given my approach; if my criticism has shaded into vitriol as times, I hope the reader will understand that my anger is rooted in a love for the Immortality Ode, not in personal animosity. A reading of the Ode such as Robinson presents us with in *Radical Literary Education* seems to me the equivalent of someone defiling a work of art; and who would hesitate to vilify an art critic who draws crude phalluses on a Rembrandt, then offers a serious critique of the disfigured picture?

My assertions about the critics' penchant for imposing their worldviews upon the Ode will, I suspect, have at times appeared hypocritical; but I hope to have made it clear that my reading does not contradict anything in Wordsworth's writings but a few suspect disclaimers in the Fenwick note. This leads me to believe that I have not *imposed* my worldview; and even if I have, I have at least counterbalanced the impositions of other critics. My argument for Wordsworth's exhibition of supersensible awareness may appear to controvert certain passages in *The Prelude,* but I am confident that the arguments I have raised to reconcile some apparently problematic passages hold good for *any* passages of this kind when objectively considered by the reader. I am equally confident that the similarities between Wordsworth and Vaughan, Traherne, and Steiner indicate their common experience, whatsoever differences among them remain, and I perceive no instance where I have *forced* Wordsworth to speak for these other writers. To return to Hoerner's figure of the critic who "weds" theory to the text, I feel justified in claiming that I have treated the bride with respect, and have not forced her to give up her faith. Mine was not an arranged marriage: I have asked her, many times, whether she will have me, and the reader may easily discern whether she has consented or not.

I think it would be a grievous error, however, to see my case as evidence for the incommensurability of worldviews, whereby a thoroughgoing materialist, for example, could never arrive at my reading. The reading I have presented is accessible to any modern reader. But for someone with a very different worldview, it would necessitate an act of sympathy and a respect for the ideas of others, even if they are long-dead authors: an act of sympathy that seems to have been lacking in the approaches of commentators on the Ode since Coleridge. Where sympathy is absent, prejudice is quick to fill in the gaps.

Clairvoyance and Reincarnation as Provisional Facts

One of my goals in this study has been to provide persons with a belief in the possibility of a prior state of existence with some genuine case studies in which a subject remembers a life before birth. It is unfortunate that Wordsworth cannot provide us with many details on this matter; he gives us little more than "trailing clouds of glory do we come / From God, who is our home." But the simplicity of his description is valuable nonetheless, for it demonstrates that he is not interested in fabricating a story, but rather in communicating an experience. Like Thomas Traherne, whose poems corroborate Wordsworth almost perfectly, he does not offer us fantastic details about the activities of the spiritual hierarchies or the achievements of a previous life, such as one meets with in many popular works on reincarnation. Traherne and Wordsworth are content to tell us what they remember, despite the difficulty of finding words that would not provoke the displeasure of unsympathetic, orthodox contemporaries. For this reason, I think that the experiences they relate should be accepted as provisional facts.

As a student of anthroposophy, I was pleasantly surprised to discover how well Wordsworth and Traherne corroborated the much more detailed clairvoyant observations of Steiner, who was very likely unfamiliar with Wordsworth and certainly unfamiliar with Traherne. The process of comparing lectures of Steiner's with passages in the Ode, and many of the poems in Traherne, was to me like encountering parallel descriptions of travellers who had explored the same unknown island, only with varying amounts of detail. And who could doubt the existence of such an island, when three independent explorers give such similar accounts? Of course, there is plenty of evidence for the veracity of Steiner's spiritual science from other quarters (see again chapter 3, n.17), but a good scholar can never have too much evidence.

A skeptic might wonder what pragmatic reasons may lead one to believe in pre-existence, if one does not in fact have memories, or inklings of memories, of the life before birth. Like all worldviews which maintain the existence of disembodied consciousness, a belief in pre-existence brings with it the corollary that there is a meaning or purpose to life; we have come here to accomplish certain things, work with certain people, suffer for past transgressions, etc. The skeptic may conclude from this pragmatic enquiry that one believes in pre-existence (or more properly, reincarnation), because it makes us feel better: we come to accept apparently unfair sources of pain as the effects of karmic justice, and we remain above the despair that comes with the feeling that all our accomplishments are ultimately dust in the wind; or that all our talents, desires, and relationships are mere accidents reducible to the activity of colliding atoms and reacting enzymes. But the belief in reincarnation does not necessarily make one feel better. When one reads of and imagines the ideal state towards which human beings ought to be progressing from life to life, and when one compares this ideal to the reality of twentieth century life, one cannot help but feel something very close to despair at the discrepancy. And so I would contend that one does not come to believe in a supersensible world and a succession of incarnations because it makes one feel better, but because these ideas accord with experience. For writers like Traherne and Wordsworth, perhaps these ideas accorded perfectly with their experience; for others, there is some room for doubt; for others, these ideas either do not accord with experience, or they simply never receive admittance into the mind as serious postulates. I hope to have supplied these latter persons with some reason to open their minds a little further in this regard.

Implications for Literary Scholarship in General

If there is an axiom to be drawn from my analysis of criticism on the Ode, it might go something like, "critics get into trouble when they do not take into account all the words in a literary work, all of its known variants, and as much relevant context from the author's *oevre* as possible." It is really quite embarrassing to see respectable Wordsworth scholars discounting the poet's positive allusions to pre-existence in *The Prelude*, or ignoring the variants of the Ode published by Curtis, or failing to see that Wordsworth's lines "Composed upon an Evening of extraordinary Splendour and Beauty" clearly indicate that whatever was lost in the Ode was briefly restored in his old age. For all my insistence that these over-sights result from doctrinal prejudice, I wonder if an equally important factor lies in a mere lack of thorough scholarship, together with an ingrained reliance on authorities—the very faults which literary criticism has, as a profession, striven so desperately to overcome in the twentieth century. Insofar as the Immortality Ode and the commentary surrounding it exemplify literary scholarship in general, it seems to me that we have achieved little since Fulgentius decided to rehabilitate the myths of ancient Greece for the service of Christian piety.

We have seen how certain positivist critics tried to rehabilitate the Ode in the name of science; the New Critical movement that began in the thir-ties tried to rehabilitate the whole study of poetry in the name of science, or at least in the name of academicism, through an emphasis on structure. By concentrating on putatively incontrovertible elements in a poem—the tensions, the ambiguities, the mechanics of metre and motif—the New Critics sought to introduce a respectable trapping of positivist hard sci-ence into their study of "false statements," as Jeremy Bentham was wont to characterise poetry. This attempt to make the study of literature more methodical (and its insights reproducible across hundreds of classrooms) seems to have enjoyed some success, but the vicissitudes of interpreta-tion—those parts of a literary work which really interest people, one might say—seem to have prevented this positivist methodology from eclipsing traditional concerns with the authors of poems and what they wanted to say or hide.

Attempts to make literary scholarship seem more like a respectable sci-ence did not stop with the structuralists, of course. A new generation of critics has arisen, the postmoderns and poststructuralists, scholars for the Age to end all Ages. These have, mainly by borrowing from French philosophers and sociologists, brought to the study of literature a whole new language, it seems, together with radical theories about the intricacies of signification. At last, the cynic might remark, literary scholars have developed a jargon as opaque as any employed by the physical and social sciences, and can mystify their undergraduates as well as any professor of physics or geology. But for all the jargon, for all the study required to master poststructuralist philosophy, and for all the opportunities to generate new theses on works that had, it seemed, been mined for all they were worth—for all this, has literary scholarship become any more of a science? Has it become more thorough, standardized, and less dependent on authority? If it is justifiable for me to make an example of the articles I have attacked in chapter 7, I would say that postmodern literary scholarship is subject to the same vagaries as its predecessors, only now the errors are more difficult to detect beneath the affectations of oracularity.

Perhaps some would contend that literary scholars are not interested in approaching the status of scientists, however impressive the financial grants to the latter may be; some would say that in literature, there are no laws and facts to discover; our domain is the indeterminate world of signification, the unconscious, the aesthetic. Certainly the detached observation demanded by science is constantly thwarted when we are faced with literature, for it engages our imagination and requires that we fill out the picture ourselves. But perhaps we can, and should, nevertheless hold it as our ideal to be as self-conscious as possible about our own contribution, our own prejudices, and our notion of what something *ought* to say. For how else can we receive new ideas and impressions, other than to compensate for the subjective interference we inevitably generate when we face them? In a way, ours is a task more difficult than that of a physical scientist. A physicist rarely needs to question his or her own role in an experiment (certain tricks with particles subject to Heisenberg's Principle excepted); the literary scholar must be much more self-conscious, more objective. This has, at any rate, been my ideal in this study. Luckily, contrary-minded readers have helped me see where I have failed to achieve it.

A Disentangled and a Naked Sence
    A Mind that's unpossest,
    A Disengaged Brest,
An Empty and a Quick Intelligence
    Acquainted with the Golden Mean,
An Even Spirit Pure and Serene,
Is that where Beauty, Excellence,
And Pleasure keep their Court of Residence

    —Thomas Traherne, "The Preparative"

Appendix

Ode: Intimations of Immortality from Recollections of Early Childhood

The Child is the father of the Man;
And I could wish my days to be
Bound each to each by natural piety.

I

THERE was a time when meadow, grove, and stream
The earth, and every common sight,
    To me did seem
    Apparelled in celestial light,
The glory and the freshness of a dream.
It is not now as it hath been of yore;—
    Turn wheresoe'er I may,
    By night or day,
The things which I have seen I now can see no more.

II

The Rainbow comes and goes,   10
And lovely is the Rose,

The Moon doth with delight
Look round her when the heavens are bare;
 Waters on a starry night
 Are beautiful and fair;
 The sunshine is a glorious birth;
 But yet I know, where'er I go,
That there hath past away a glory from the earth.

III

Now, while yet the birds thus sing a joyous song,
 And while the young lambs bound   20
 As to the tabor's sound,
To me alone there came a thought of grief:
A timely utterance gave that thought relief,
 And I again am strong:
The cataracts blow their trumpets from the steep;
No more shall grief of mine the season wrong;
I hear the Echoes through the mountains throng,
The Winds come to me from the fields of sleep,
 And all the earth is gay;
   Land and sea   30
 Give themselves up to jollity,
 And with the heart of May
 Doth every Beast keep holiday;—
  Thou Child of Joy,
Shout round me, let me hear thy shouts, thou happy Shepherd-boy!

IV

Ye blessèd Creatures, I have heard the call
 Ye to each other make; I see
The heavens laugh with you in your jubilee;
 My heart is at your festival,

My head hath its coronal, 40
The fulness of your bliss, I feel—I feel it all.
    Oh evil day! If I were sullen
    While Earth herself is adorning,
    This sweet May-morning,
    And the Children are culling
    On every side,
    In a thousand valleys far and wide,
    Fresh flowers; while the sun shines warm,
And the Babe leaps up on his Mother's arm:—
    I hear, I hear, with joy I hear! 50
—But there's a Tree, of many, one,
A single Field which I have looked upon,
Both of them speak of something that is gone:
    The Pansy at my feet
    Doth the same tale repeat:
Whither is fled the visionary gleam?
Where is it now, the glory and the dream?

            V
Our birth is but a sleep and a forgetting:
The Soul that rises with us, our life's Star,
    Hath had elsewhere its setting, 60
    And cometh from afar:
    Not in entire forgetfulness,
    And not in utter nakedness,
    But trailing clouds of glory do we come
    From God, who is our home:
Heaven lies about us in our infancy!
Shades of the prison-house begin to close
    Upon the growing Boy,
        But He

Beholds the light, and whence it flows,   70
    He sees it in his joy;
The Youth, who daily farther from the east
    Must travel, still is Nature's Priest,
    And by the vision splendid
    Is on his way attended;
At length the Man perceives it die away,
And fade into the light of common day.

VI

Earth fills her lap with pleasures of her own;
Yearnings she hath in her own natural kind,
And, even with something of a Mother's mind, 80
    And no unworthy aim,
    The homely Nurse doth all she can
To make her Foster-child, her Inmate Man,
    Forget the glories he hath known,
And that imperial palace whence he came.

VII

Behold the Child among his new-born blisses,
A six-years' Darling of a pigmy size!
See, where 'mid work of his own hand he lies,
Fretted by sallies of his mother's kisses,
With a light upon him from his father's eyes!   90
See, at his feet, some little plan or chart,
Some fragment from his dream of human life,
Shaped by himself with newly-learned art;
    A wedding or a festival,
    A mourning or a funeral;
     And this hath now his heart,
    And unto this he frames his song:

Then will he fit his tongue
To dialogues of business, love, or strife;
But it will not be long 100
Ere this be thrown aside,
And with new joy and pride
The little Actor cons another part;
Filling from time to time his "humorous stage"
With all the Persons, down to palsied Age,
That Life brings with her in her equipage;
As if his whole vocation
Were endless imitation.

VIII
Thou, whose exterior semblance doth belie
Thy Soul's immensity; 110
Thou best Philosopher, who yet dost keep
Thy heritage, thou Eye among the blind,
That, deaf and silent, read'st the eternal deep,
Haunted for ever by the eternal mind,—
Mighty Prophet! Seer blest!
On whom those truths do rest,
Which we are toiling all our lives to find,
In darkness lost, the darkness of the grave;
Thou, over whom thy Immortality
Broods like the Day, a Master o'er a Slave, 120
A Presence which is not to be put by;
Thou little Child, yet glorious in the might
Of heaven-born freedom on thy being's height,
Why with such earnest pains dost thou provoke
The years to bring the inevitable yoke,
Thus blindly with thy blessedness at strife?
Full soon thy Soul shall have her earthly freight,

And custom lie upon thee with a weight,
Heavy as frost, and deep almost as life!

IX

O joy! That in our embers   130
Is something that yet doth live,
That nature yet remembers
What was so fugitive!
The thought of our past years in me doth breed
Perpetual benediction: not indeed
For that which is most worthy to be blest;
Delight and liberty, the simple creed
Of Childhood, whether busy or at rest,
With new-fledged hope still fluttering in his breast:—
Not for these I raise   140
The song of thanks and praise;
But for those obstinate questionings
Of sense and outward things,
Fallings from us, vanishings;
Blank misgivings of a Creature
Moving about in worlds not realised,
High instincts before which our mortal Nature
Did tremble like a guilty Thing surprised:
But for those first affections,
Those shadowy recollections,   150
Which, be they what they may,
Are yet the fountain light of all our day,
Are yet the master light of all our seeing;
Uphold us, cherish, and have the power to make
Our noisy years seem moments in the being
Of the eternal Silence: truths that wake,
To perish never;

Which neither listlessness, nor mad endeavour,
    Nor Man nor Boy,
Nor all that is at enmity with joy,   160
Can utterly abolish or destroy.
Hence in a season of calm weather
    Though inland far we be,
Our Souls have sight of that immortal sea
    Which brought us hither,
    Can in a moment travel thither,
And see the Children sport upon the shore,
And hear the mighty waters rolling evermore.

        X
Then sing, ye Birds, sing, sing a joyous song!
    And let the young Lambs bound   170
    As to the tabor's sound!
We in thought will join your throng,
    Ye that pipe and ye that play,
    Ye that through your hearts to-day
    Feel the gladness of the May!
What though the radiance which was once so bright
Be now for ever taken from my sight,
    Though nothing can bring back the hour
Of splendour in the grass, of glory in the flower;
    We will grieve not, rather find   180
    Strength in what remains behind;
    In the primal sympathy
    Which having been must ever be;
    In the soothing thoughts that spring
    Out of human suffering;
    In the faith that looks through death,
In years that bring the philosophic mind.

XI

And O, ye Fountains, Meadows, Hills, and Groves,
Forebode not any severing of our loves!
Yet in my heart of hearts I feel your might; 190
I only have relinquished one delight
To live beneath your more habitual sway.
I love the Brooks which down their channels fret,
Even more than when I tripped as lightly as they;
The innocent brightness of a new-born Day
    Is lovely yet;
The Clouds that gather round the setting sun
Do take a sober colouring from an eye
That hath kept watch o'er man's mortality;
Another race hath been, and other palms are won. 200
Thanks to the human heart by which we live,
Thanks to its tenderness, its joys, and fears,
To me the meanest flower that blows can give
Thoughts that do often lie too deep for tears.

Notes

Chapter 1

1. Gene Ruoff, arguing the unimportance of immortality and pre-existence to the Ode, finds stanzas 5-8 "repetitive" rather than "developmental" (251). The myth, he claims, "attempts the darkest possible reading of the Ode's early stanzas"; it does not offer the speaker consolation "but impedes it, and finally makes that recovery the more significant by increasing the enormity of the obstacles that have been overcome" (251-52). Peter Manning sees a similar tension: "[t]he absent, lost heritage with which [Wordsworth] aligns himself intensifies his unease: his "Immortality" "broods" over him… (86).

2. As W. K. Wimsatt and Monroe Beardsley declared, "[c]ritical inquiries are not settled by consulting the oracle," even if the oracle is the author (951).

3. *Biographia Literaria* 2.147. I discuss the questionable influences of Coleridge in chapter 5.

4. Lines 58-61. Unless otherwise indicated, quotations of Wordsworth's poems (except *The Prelude*) are from de Selincourt's *The Poetical Works of William Wordsworth*. (I cite the full text of the Immortality Ode as an appendix). Although the Cornell Wordsworth series generally offers a much better critical tool for studying Wordsworth, the de Selincourt collections are generally more accessible. The reading text of the Ode prepared by the Cornell editors also includes some choices which are at odds with the reading presented here.

5. The letter is quoted at the end of chapter 4.

6. Hoffpauir, approaching the Ode in the spirit of Yvor Winters, finds Wordsworth "not only complacent, but insincere" in the didactic movements of the Ode (79).

7. Unless otherwise indicated, references are to the 1805 edition.

8.   Reluctantly to England I returned
   Compelled by nothing less than absolute want
   Of funds for my support; else, well assured
   That I both was and must be of small worth,
   No better than an alien in the land.... (*Prelude* 10.189-93)

9. "Essay upon Epitaphs" 53. Curiously, this passage is quoted by E. D. Hirsch in *Wordsworth and Schelling* (162) and John Beer in *Wordsworth in Time* (173-74), but both Hirsch and Beer seem to miss its import entirely.

10. "I confess, with me the conviction is absolute, that, if the impression and sense of death were not thus [i.e., through intimations of immortality] counterbalanced, such a hollowness would pervade the whole system of things, such a want of correspondence and consistency, a disproportion so astounding betwixt means and ends, that there could be no repose, no joy" ("Essay upon Epitaphs" 52).

Chapter 2

1. Stace 132. Rudolf Steiner, whose more articulate thoughts on mysticism will be deferred to chapter 3, comments that unity and multiplicity are in any case useless concepts in the spiritual world, since "[i]t is unity and multiplicity at the same time" (*Esoteric Development* 167).

2. One of these end-stops is omitted in the Norton *Prelude*, without, I believe, any justification from the mss. Lines 254-55 in the Norton read "Tenacious of the forms which it receives / In one beloved presence," whereas Dove Cottage ms. 52 (*Prelude* ms. A) has a period after "receives." The de Selincourt *Prelude* also includes the period.

3. That his doubt is about whether he owes something to the "beauteous forms" (line 22) is clear from lines 35ff.:

> Nor less, I trust,
> To them I may have owed another gift,
> Of aspect more sublime; that blessed mood
> In which the burthen of the mystery,
> In which the heavy and the weary weight
> Of all this unintelligible world,
> Is lightened:—that serene and blessed mood,
> In which the affections gently lead us on,—
> Until, the breath of this corporeal frame
> And even the motion of our human blood
> Almost suspended, we are laid asleep
> In body, and become a living soul:
> While with an eye made quiet by the power
> Of harmony, and the deep power of joy,
> We see into the life of things.
> If this
> Be but a vain belief, yet oh! how oft...
> How oft, in spirit, have I turned to thee,
> O sylvan Wye!... (35-56)

4. Lines 61-80. For the reader unable to make the connection, Wordsworth included a note stating that "allusions to the Ode entitled

'Intimations of Immortality' pervade the last Stanza of the foregoing poem"

    (*PW* 4. 13).

5. Ruskin 5.369; Trilling 137; Ross 635; Levinson 102.

6. I quote Taylor's observations at the end of chapter 4.

Chapter 3

1. "Henry Vaughan may stand... as a writer with whom Wordsworth was almost certainly acquainted" (Ruoff 256).

2. The biographical character of the Immortality Ode is ascertainable from Wordsworth's comments about it, and the confessional nature of Vaughan's poetry is easily inferred; I do not believe he ever speaks *in persona*.

3. Bucke's experience is quoted on page 18 above.

4. Traherne did actually publish a few tracts in his lifetime, but these quickly fell into obscurity. These consisted of *Roman Forgeries*, an attack on Roman Catholic apologists; and *Christian Ethicks*, "a work of exalted but confused piety" (Hayward iii). Several other of his devotional prose works were published anonymously, but none of his poetry.

5. Lines 1-8. Quotations of Traherne's poetry refer to the Dobell manuscript versions in *The Poetical Works of Thomas Traherne*, excepting poems that exist only in the *Poems of Felicity* versions.

6. Lehrs suggests that Dobell is wrong in citing this poem as evidence of Traherne's "Berkeleian" philosophy, since the infant's perceptions

extend beyond the sensible, while Berkeley's idealism concerned only the sensible world as mind-picture. See Lehrs, *Man or Matter*, 151-53.

7. The manuscript was discovered in 1967 but not identified until 1981.

8. EEGs (electroencephalograms) are records of "electrical field potentials that can be picked up from the surface of the scalp" (Eccles, *The Human Psyche* 80). Different states of consciousness and mental activity generate EEGs (also called "brain waves") of varying magnitude and regularity; curiously, the best conditions for generating brain waves are "when there is minimal mental activity" (Eccles, *Human Psyche* 81).

9. The possibilities that the note was fabricated or that the mother and daughter were conspiring to send medical science a pro-life message seem to me unlikely for several reasons: first, Dee's back pain disappeared after the surfacing of the memory, which suggests a psychosomatic effect that can scarcely be ascribed to her making up a story; second, I cannot imagine why someone wishing to advance the cause of pro-life would expend so much time and money trying to convince *one* doctor, who at that time had published no articles on early memory, of the sentience of fetuses.

10. Chamberlain cites Josephine Van Husen, Graham Farrant, and a Canadian psychologist, Andrew Feldmar.

11. Eccles is perhaps best known for having co-authored *The Self and its Brain* with Karl Popper.

12. Sheldrake 371. Sheldrake's hypothesis is mainly concerned with explaining the appearance of organic form, for which the idea of "genetic programs" is an inadequate explanation; all cells in a body are genetically identical, "[y]et they have different shapes. Clearly, the genes alone cannot explain these differences" (Sheldrake 86). He also makes it clear that explanations of coordinated animal behaviour such as schooling and flocking necessitate something like morphic fields (231-36).

13. An abridged version of Head and Cranston's list would include the Mandingo, Zulu, and Bantu of Africa; the Arunta, Warramunga, and Urabunna of Australia; the Tahitians, Solomon Islanders, and Maori of Oceania; the Dravidians and Nayars of India; the Karens, Giliaks, and Cheremiss of Asia; the Algonquin, Dene, and Haida of North America; the Icanne and Abysone of South America; and the Finns, Danes, Celts, and Lombards of Europe.

14. Accessible introductions to his work may be found in *The Essential Steiner*, ed. Robert McDermott (San Francisco: Harper and Row, 1984); Rudi Lissau's Rudolf Steiner (Stroud, U.K.: Hawthorn Press, 1987); and in Stuart C. Easton's *Man and World in the Light of Anthroposophy* (Spring Valley, NY: Anthroposophic Press, 1975).

15. Steiner's background is available in *Rudolf Steiner, An Autobiography*. He is at pains in this book to show his independence from the spiritual teachings of the Theosophists (a group with which W. B. Yeats was associated), even though he was the head of the Theosophical Society in Germany for a brief period.

16. A full treatment of Steiner's epistemological justifications for supersensible research is provided in *An Outline of Occult Science* 3-20.

17. Steiner designed the original curriculum of Waldorf school education, which is practiced in most European countries, as well as many other countries around the world; a number of physicians worldwide practice anthroposophical medicine; Steiner's lectures on agriculture have led to the Bio-Dynamic farming method, also practiced internationally; and Paul Schatz, a Swiss engineer and geometrician, developed the geometrical principle of the "inversion kinetic" out of a mere suggestion of Steiner's "that if someone took the trouble to investigate the dynamics of the relationship between the Zodiac and the five Platonic solids, especially the cube, something of great importance in the realm of motion (kinetics) would be discovered" (Cruse 13). The inversion kinetic has since been applied to mixing machine technology; among other properties, the kinetic "appears to be the optimum motion for the mixing of free-flowing ingredients" (Cruse 13).

18. Typical are the descriptions of these worlds given throughout *Occult Science.*

19. Although Steiner was a Goethe scholar and steeped in the philosophy and literature of the nineteenth century, his writings and lectures cannot be assembled from this milieu. He is in fact too ready to draw parallels between his observations and Goethe's writings in the few cases where this is possible, and probably would have been proud to claim more parallels did these exist. Steiner's critics did attack him for presenting as observations ideas extant in gnostic writings, however, for which he offers a defense: "the results of my perception stood before me. They were, at the outset, "perceptions" without names. Were I to communicate them, I needed verbal designations. I then sought later for such designations in older descriptions of the spiritual in order to be able to express in words what was still wordless. I employed these verbal designations freely, so

that in my use of them scarcely *one* coincides with its ancient meaning (*Occult Science* xv).

20. Head and Cranston provide some information about the Mystery Schools of ancient Greece, which are "believed to be copies of the more ancient Indian and Egyptian Mysteries" (194). Secret teachings were apparently encoded in dramas: "[t]he pre-existent condition of the spirit and soul was symbolized; the lapse of the latter into earth life and Hades; the long wanderings through many lives; the gradual purification of the soul and its eventual reunion with spirit.

    "At Eleusis the familiar story of Demeter and Persephone was portrayed, signifying, according to Sallust, the periodical descent of souls.... In the Orphic Mysteries, Bacchus torn to pieces by the Titans and then made whole again, was dramatized. Plutarch calls this 'a sacred narrative concerning reincarnation'" (Head 194-95). Steiner seems to be referring to Mystery Schools in general.

21. *Esoteric Development* 94. Steiner remarks that Imagination is a controlled form of what is known today as near-death experience: "[a] phenomenon that has often been described by people who have been at the point of drowning, namely that they see their life backwards in a series of moving pictures, can be deliberately and systematically cultivated so that one can see all the events of the present earthly life" (*Es. Dev.* 88).

Chapter 4

1. *Letters* 174; qtd. in *Poetical Works* 4.464.

2. Ruoff claims that the supersensible pre-existence introduced in stanza 5 is not necessary "to explain the phenomena which had generated the Ode of 1802" (233).

3. See Rea, "Coleridge's Intimations of Immortality from Proclus" 208.

4. Diary entry, 8 August 1811; qtd. in *Books and Their Writers* 1.44; qtd. in McFarland 65.

5. Letter from Bonamy Price to William Knight, April 21, 1881; qtd. in *Poetical Works* 4.467 n.

6. Wordsworth suspects the same of his daughter Caroline in the "Beauteous Evening" sonnet (Sonnet XXX of the Miscellaneous sonnets) when he thinks of her as residing in "Abraham's bosom," i.e., with God, "all the year" (line 12). I connect this sonnet to the Ode further in my discussion, on page 86, of the shore-ocean figure.

7. I am not certain what the theologians have to say about this, but it is certainly the way souls are represented in Christian art, which probably follows the example of the corpse-sized souls in Virgil's Hades.

8. "The ego—with the whole of man's core of being—can be viewed as an entity which experiences its relationship to the objective world within that world itself, and receives its experiences as reflections in the form of impressions from the bodily organization.... Since the ordinary consciousness, in the sense of the epistemological considerations here presented, is rendered possible only through the reflection (through the reflected representations), it ceases, therefore during the state of sleep. The condition of mind of the spiritual researcher can be understood as one in which the illusion of ordinary consciousness is overcome, and which gains a starting point in the life of soul from which it actually experiences the human core of being in free release from the bodily organization" (*Esoteric Development* 53).

9. For example, Paul Fry discovers in the figure the sense of an oppressive father god for whom "Immortality" stands metonymically: "for the child's domination by Mother Earth, then, there is an equivalent master-slave dialectic between son and father. Immortal regions are suddenly as much like prisons as mortal ones..." (62-63).

10. Kenneth R. Johnston takes this stand in "Recollecting Forgetting: Forcing Paradox to the Limit in the 'Intimations Ode'"; and Charles Sherry makes a similar argument in *Wordsworth's Poetry of the Imagination* 1-31.

11. By reading Wordsworth's "unconscious intercourse" in this way, we can dissolve the contradiction that the Norton editors, following R. D. Havens, find in *Prelude* 1.609-40. Because of their failure to see that Wordsworth speaks of spiritual things in terms of and together with material things, the editors cannot see how the "'Gleams like the flashing of a shield' are positively 'felt' in *1805*, 613-14... but natural 'objects and appearances' in *1805*, 621-23... are 'lifeless,' and 'doomed to sleep / Until maturer seasons [call] them forth'" (62 n. 3):

> [E]ven then I felt
> Gleams like the flashing of a shield. The earth
> And common face of Nature spake to me
> Rememberable things; sometimes, 'tis true,
> By chance collisions and quaint accidents—
> Like those ill-sorted unions, work supposed
> Of evil-minded fairies—yet not in vain
> Nor profitless, if haply they impressed
> Collateral objects and appearances,
> Albeit lifeless then, and doomed to sleep

Until maturer seasons called them forth
To impregnate and to elevate the mind. (613-624)

Obviously, if the "Gleams like the flashing of a smiled" are distinct from 'natural objects and appearances,' one may be "felt" while the other is "doomed to sleep."

12. *Five Books of Plotinus* (London, 1794) lvi-lvii; qtd. in Irene Chayes, "Coleridge, Metempsychosis, and 'Almost all the Followers of Fenelon'" 296-97.

13. Letter to Mrs. Clarkson, Jan. 15, 1815, *Letters* 174.

Chapter 5

1. Margaret Oliphant, *The Literary History of England* (London: 1882) 1.328; qtd. in Barbara Garlitz, "The Immortality Ode: Its Cultural Progeny" 639.

2. As Coleridge proclaims at the end of the *Biographia*, it has been his "Object" to "kindle young minds… by showing that the Scheme of Christianity, as taught in the Liturgy and Homilies of our Church, though not discoverable by human Reason, is yet in accordance with it…" (2.247).

3. See chapter 4 above.

4. See Plato, *Republic* 621a-b: "Now, [the souls] were all required to drink a certain amount of water, but some were too stupid to look after themselves properly and drank more than the required amount. As each person drank, he forgot everything. They lay down to sleep, and in the middle of the night there was thunder and an earthquake. All of a sudden, they were lifted up from where they were, and they

darted like shooting stars away in various directions for rebirth. As for Er, although he hadn't been allowed to drink any of the water he had no idea what direction he took, or how he got back to his body, but he suddenly opened his eyes and found that it was early in the morning and that he was lying on the funeral pyre."

5. *Biographia Literaria* 2.141. Coleridge is criticizing Wordsworth's lines, excised after 1820, in which the child is addressed as believing "the grave / Is but a lonely bed without the sense or sight / Of day or the warm light, / A place of thought where we in waiting lie" (120-23). That Wordsworth seems to have believed this as a child, and perhaps even as an adult, seems to me to proceed from a certainty of consciousness after death that is unreconciled to teachings of the Last Judgment. On the other hand, it is possible that by "grave" he means earthly life, where "we in waiting lie" for our immortality.

6. Letter to Thelwall, Nov. 19, 1796 (*Collected Letters* 1.260). The occasion for the sonnet was Coleridge's anxiety, that his son (Hartley) might die at birth. The implication is that if the child were a spirit incarnating, "Sentenc'd for some more venial crime to grieve," the pain of birth would have been sufficient atonement, and his death met with "Heaven's quick reprieve" (lines 12-14).

7. *Notes on English Divines* 2.263; qtd. in Perkins 19.

8. Coleridge mentions his early interest in Proclus and Plotinus in *Biographia Literaria*, 1.144.

9. *Philosophical Lectures* 317. I preserve for comic effect Coburn's small capitals, which she uses to distinguish material taken from Coleridge's notes.

10. *Edinburgh Review* 14 (April 1809) 187ff.; qtd. in Raine 23.

11. Apparently recognizing herself as belonging to this school, Anya Taylor elaborates Coleridge's instructions: "Only those few readers who 'feel a deep interest in modes of inmost being' will find stanzas V and IX 'intelligible'.... These few are the same few tremulous spirits for whom the *Biographia* itself will have meaning as a spiritual guide" (640).

12. *Aids to Reflection* 389. Compare John Locke's *Essay Concerning Human Understanding*: "their minds being thus prepared, whatever groundless opinion comes to settle itself strongly upon their fancies is an illumination from the Spirit of God, and presently of divine authority; and whatsoever odd action they find in themselves a strong inclination to do, that impulse is concluded to be a call or direction from heaven and must be obeyed.... This I take to be properly enthusiasm..." (4.19.6-7)

13. *BL* 141. See for discussion of the grave passage note 5 above.

14. It is unfortunate that Wordsworth could not recall for his defence the evidence *for* pre-existence's according with revelation, namely Christ's avowal that John the Baptist was Elijah (Matt. 11.13-15).

Chapter 6

1. *Letters of John Stuart Mill*, ed. H. S. R. Elliot (London, 1910) 2.358; qtd. in Abrams, "Belief and Disbelief" 119.

2. Stephen 259. No source is provided by Stephen for his quotation.

Chapter 7

1. I have cited several of these elsewhere. See pages 1, 67, 89.

2. I feel justified in speaking of a cult here not only because of the hundreds of recent scholarly articles dealing with representations of "the body," but owing to current popular obsessions with fitness, body-building, body-piercing, etc.

3. I quote Hazlitt's essay at length on page 13, above; qtd. in Robinson, *Radical Literary Education*, 160-61.

4. Lines 9-16. De Selincourt's *Poetical Works* does not include the poem; it appears, however, in John Haydon's edition of *The Poems* 421-22.

5. Curtis notes this variant in his reading text (276).

6. "[B]y transposing the Letters of the Alphabet, in any suspected Paper, they can lay open the deepest Designs of a discontented Party. So for Example, if I should say in a Letter to a Friend, *Our Brother* Tom *has just got the Piles*; a Man of Skill in this Art would discover how the same Letters which compose that Sentence, may be analysed into the following words; *Resist,——a Plot is brought home——The Tour*. And this is the Anagrammatick Method." See *Gulliver's Travels* 191-92.

References

Primary

Browning, Elizabeth Barrett. "A Child Asleep." In *Poems by Elizabeth Barrett Browning*. London: Smith and Elder, 1902, p. 243-45.

—. *Aurora Leigh*. In *The Complete Works of Elizabeth Barrett Browning*. Ed. Charlotte Porter and Helen Clarke. Vol. 4. New York: AMS Press, 1973. 6 vols.

Coleridge, Samuel Taylor. *Aids to Reflection*. Ed. John Beer. *The Collected Works of Samuel Taylor Coleridge* 9. Gen ed. Kathleen Coburn. Princeton: Princeton UP, 1993.

—. *Biographia Literaria*. Ed. James Engell and W. Jackson Bate. *The Collected Works* 7; 2 vols. Princeton: Princeton UP, 1983.

—. *The Collected Letters of Samuel Taylor Coleridge*. Ed. Earl Leslie Griggs. 6 vols. Oxford: Clarendon, 1956-1971.

—. *The Notebooks of Samuel Taylor Coleridge*. Ed. Kathleeen Coburn. Vol. 3, pt. 1: Text. Princeton: Princeton UP, 1973. 5 vols.

—. *The Philosophical Lectures of Samuel Taylor Coleridge*. Ed. Kathleen Coburn. New York: Philosophical Library, 1949.

Milton, John. *Paradise Lost*. Ed. Scott Elledge. 2nd ed. New York: Norton, 1993.

Traherne, Thomas. *The Poetical Works of Thomas Traherne*. Ed. Gladys I. Wade. New York: Cooper Square, 1965.

—. *Centuries of Meditations*. 1908. Ed. Bertram Dobell. London: Robert Stockwell, 1950.

—. "Ages II." In *Commentaries of Heaven: The Poems*. Ed. D. D. C. Chambers. Elizabethan and Renaissance Studies Series 92:22. Gen. ed. James Hogg. Salzburg: Institut für Anglisitik und Amerikanistik, 1989.

Vaughan, Henry. "The Retreat." In *Silex Scintillans 1650*. Menston: Scolar Press, 1968, p. 34.

—. "Vanity of Spirit." In *Silex Scintillans 1650*, p. 33.

Wordsworth, William. "Essay upon Epitaphs, I." In *The Prose Works of William Wordsworth*. Ed. W. J. B. Owen and Jane Worthington Smyser. Vol. 2. Oxford: Clarendon, 1974.

—. *Poems in Two Volumes, and Other Poems, 1800-1807*. Ed. Jared R. Curtis. The Cornell Wordsworth Series. Ithaca, N.Y.: Cornell University Press, 1983.

—. *The Poetical Works of William Wordsworth*. Ed. Ernest de Selincourt. Oxford: Clarendon, 1949. 5 vols.

—. *The Poems*. Ed. John O. Hayden. New Haven; London: Yale UP, 1981. 2 vols.

—. *The Prelude*; or, Growth of a Poet's Mind. Ed. Ernest de Selincourt. 2nd ed. rev. London: Oxford University Press, 1960.

—. *The Prelude: 1799, 1805, 1850.* Ed. Jonathan Wordsworth, M. H. Abrams, and Stephen Gill. New York: Norton, 1979.

—. *Letters of William Wordsworth: A New Selection.* Ed. Alan G. Hill. Oxford: Oxford, 1984.

Secondary

Abrams, M. H. "Belief and Disbelief." *UTQ* 22 (1958): 117-35.

Beer, John. *Wordsworth in Time.* London: Faber and Faber, 1979.

Berkeley, George. *The Works of George Berkeley.* Ed. Alexander Fraser. Oxford: Clarendon, 1901. 4 vols.

Blavatsky, H. P. *The Secret Doctrine.* London: Theosophical Publishing, 1893. 4 vols.

Brooks, Cleanth. *The Well-Wrought Urn: Studies in the Structure of Poetry.* New York: Harcourt Brace Jovanovich, 1974.

Bucke, Richard Maurice. *Cosmic Consciousness: A Study in the Evolution of the Human Mind.* New York: Citadel Press, 1970.

Burke, Edmund. *Reflections on the Revolution in France.* In *Eighteenth-century English Literature.* Ed. Geoffrey Tillotson et al. New York: Harcourt, Brace and World, 1969. 1270-88.

Chamberlain, David. "The Expanding Boundaries of Memory." *Pre- and Peri-Natal Psychology* 4.3 (1990): 171-89.

Chayes, Irene. "Coleridge, Metempsychosis, and 'almost all the followers of Fenelon'." *ELH* 25 (1958): 290-315.

Cheek, David. "Are Telepathy, Clairvoyance, and 'Hearing' Possible in Utero? Suggestive Evidence as Revealed During Hypnotic Age-Regression Studies of Prenatal Memory." *Pre- and Perinatal Psychology Journal* 7.2 (1992): 125-137.

Clark, Elizabeth A. *The Origenist Controversy: The Cultural Construction of an Early Christian Debate.* Princeton: Princeton UP, 1992.

Cruse, Don. "The Industrial Legacy of Paul Schatz." *What is happening in the Anthroposophical Society* Mar. 1994: 13-14.

Curran, Stuart. "Romantic Poetry: Why and Wherefore?" In *The Cambridge Companion to British Romanticism.* Cambridge; New York: Cambridge UP, 1993. 216-35.

Curtis, Jared. "The Best Philosopher: New Variants for Wordsworth's Immortality Ode." *YULG* 44 (1970): 139-47.

Dobell, Bertram. Introduction. In *The Poetical Works of Thomas Traherne.* By Thomas Traherne. Ed. Gladys I. Wade. New York: Cooper Square, 1965, xxii-xciii.

Eccles, John C. *How the Self Controls its Brain*. Berlin: Springer-Verlag, 1994.

—. *The Human Psyche*. Berlin: Springer International, 1980.

Edmundson, Mark. "Vital Intimations: Wordsworth, Coleridge, and the Promise of Criticism." *SAQ* 91 (1992): 739-64.

Fry, Paul. "Wordworth's Severe Intimations." In *The Poet's Calling in the English Ode*. Boston: Yale UP, 1980. Rpt. in *Critical Essays on William Wordsworth*. Ed. George Gilpin. Boston: G. K. Hall, 1990, 55-82.

Fulgentius. *Fulgentius the Mythographer*. Trans. Leslie G. Whitbread. Columbus: Ohio State UP, 1971.

Gardner, Edmund. *Dante and the Mystics: A Study of the Mystical Aspect of the Divina Commedia and its Relations with some of its Mediaeval Sources*. New York: Octagon Books, 1968.

Garlitz, Barbara. "The Immortality Ode: Its Cultural Progeny." *SEL* 6 (1966): 639-49.

Garrod, H. W. *Wordsworth: Lectures and Essays*. Oxford: Clarendon, 1927.

Gravil, Richard. "Coleridge's Wordworth." *The Wordsworth Circle* 15 (1984): 17-19.

Grob, Alan. *The Philosophic Mind: A Study of Wordsworth's Poetry and Thought, 1797 1805*. Columbus: Ohio State UP, 1973.

Hartman, Geoffrey. *The Unremarkable Wordsworth*. Minneapolis: U of Minnesota P, 1987.

Hayward, John. Introduction. *Centuries of Meditations.* By Thomas Traherne. London: Robert Stockwell, 1950. Not paginated.

Hazlitt, William. "Romeo and Juliet." In *Selected Writings.* Ed. Ronald Blythe. Harmondsworth: Penguin, 1970. 279-83.

Head, Joseph, and S. L. Cranston. *Reincarnation in World Thought.* New York: Julian Press, 1967.

Hirsch, Eric D. *Wordsworth and Schelling: A Typological Study of Romanticism.* New Haven: Yale UP, 1960.

Hoerner, Fred. "Nostalgia's Freight in Wordsworth's *Intimations Ode.*" *ELH* 62 (1995): 631-61.

Hoffpauir, Richard. *Romantic Fallacies.* New York: Peter Lang, 1986.

Johnston, Kenneth R. "Recollecting Forgetting: Forcing Paradox to the Limit in the 'Intimations Ode'." *TWC* 2 (1971): 59-64.

Lehrs, Ernst. *Man or Matter: Introduction to a Spiritual Understanding of Nature on the Basis of Goethe's Method of Training Observation and Thought.* 2nd ed. London: Faber & Faber, 1958.

Levinson, Marjorie. "The Intimations Ode: A Timely Utterance." In *Wordsworth's Great Period Poems: Four Essays.* London: Cambridge UP, 1986. Rpt. in *Critical Essays on William Wordsworth.* Ed. George Gilpin. Boston: G. K. Hall, 1990, 55-82.

Leyburn, Ellen Douglass. "Berkeleian Elements in Wordsworth's Thought." *JEGP* 47 (1948): 14-28.

Locke, John. *An Essay Concerning Human Understanding.* Ed. John Yolton. 2 vols. London: Dent; New York: Dutton, 1964.

Magnuson, Paul. "The Genesis of Wordworth's 'Ode'." *TWC* 12 (1981): 23-30

Malekin, Peter. "Wordsworth and the Mind of Man." In *An Infinite Complexity: Essays in Romanticism.* Ed. J. R. Watson. Edinburgh: Edinburgh UP, 1983, 1-25.

Manning, Peter. "Wordsworth's Immortality Ode and its Epigraphs." *JEGP* 82 (1983): 526-40. Rpt. in *Critical Essays on William Wordsworth.* Ed. George Gilpin. Boston: G. K. Hall, 1990, 83-97.

Mathison, John K. "Wordsworth's Ode: Intimations of Immortality from Recollections of Early Childhood." *Studies in Philology* 46 (1949): 419-39.

McFarland, Thomas. "Wordsworth's Best Philosopher." *TWC* 13 (1982): 59-68.

Merrill, L. R. "Vaughan's Influence upon Wordworth's Poetry." *MLN* 37 (1922): 91-96.

Meyer, George. "A Note on the Sources and Symbolism of the Intimations Ode." *Tulane Studies in English* 3 (1952): 5-31.

Mill, J. S. *Autobiography.* 1850. Ed. Jack Stillinger. Boston: Houghton Mifflin, 1969.

Newlyn, Lucy. "The Little Actor and his Mock Apparel." *TWC* 14 (1983): 30-39.

Penfield, Wilder. *The Mystery of the Mind: A Critical Study of Consciousness and the Human Brain.* Princeton: Princeton UP, 1975.

Perkins, Mary Anne. *Coleridge's Philosophy: The Logos as Unifying Principle.* Oxford: Clarendon, 1994.

Pipkin, James W. "Wordsworth's 'Immortality Ode' and the Myth of the Fall." *Renascence* 30 (1978): 91-98.

Plato. *Phaedo.* Trans. David Gallop. Oxford: Clarendon, 1975.

—. Republic. Trans. Robin Waterfield. Oxford: New York: Oxford UP, 1993.

Proffit, Edward. "'Though inland far we be': Intimations of Evolution in the Great Ode." *TWC* 13 (1982): 88-90.

Quasten, Johannes. *Patrology.* 4 vols. Westminster, Md.: Christian Classics, 1983-1986.

Raine, Kathleen. "Thomas Taylor in England." In *Thomas Taylor the Platonist: Selected Writings.* Ed. Kathleen Raine and George M. Harper. Princeton: Princeton UP, 1969, 3-48.

Raysor, Thomas M. "Coleridge's Criticism of Wordsworth." *PMLA* 54 (1939): 496-510.

—. "The Themes of Immortality and Natural Piety in Wordsworth's Immortality Ode." *PMLA* 69 (1954): 861-75.

Rea, John D. "Coleridge's Intimations of Immortality from Proclus." *Modern Philology* 26 (1928): 201-213.

Richards, I. A. *Coleridge on Imagination*. 1934. London: Routledge and Kegan Paul, 1950.

Robinson, Henry Crabb. *Henry Crabb Robinson on Books and their Writers*. Ed. Edith J. Morley. London: Dent and Sons, 1938. 3 vols.

Robinson, Jeffrey C. "The Immortality Ode: Lionel Trilling and Helen Vendler." *TWC* 12 (1981): 89-91.

—. *Radical Literary Education: A Classroom Experiment with Wordsworth's "Ode."* Madison: U of Wisconsin P, 1987.

Rogers, David. "God and Pre-existence in Wordsworth's *Immortality Ode*." *Durham University Journal* 30 (1969): 143-46.

Ross, Daniel W. "Seeking a Way Home: The Uncanny in Wordsworth's 'Immortality Ode'." *SEL* 32 (1992): 625-43.

Ruoff, Gene. *Wordsworth and Coleridge: The Making of the Major Lyrics, 1802-04*. New Brunswick, NJ: Rutgers UP, 1989.

Ruskin, John. *Modern Painters*. In *The Complete Works of John Ruskin*. Ed. E. T. Cook and Alexander Wedderburn. Vols. 3-7. London: George Allen; New York: Longmans, Green, and Co., 1904. 39 vols.

Shaver, Chester L., and Alice C. *Wordsworth's Library; A Catalogue, Including a List of Books housed by Wordsworth for Coleridge from c.1810 to c.1830*. New York: Garland, 1979.

Sheldrake, Rupert. *The Presence of the Past: Morphic Resonance and the Habits of Nature*. London: Collins, 1988.

Sherry, Charles. *Wordsworth's Poetry of the Imagination*. Oxford: Clarendon; New York: Oxford UP, 1980.

Solomon, Gerald. "Wordsworth and the Art of Lying." *Essays in Criticism* 27 (1977): 141-56.

Stace, W. T. *Mysticism and Philosophy*. London: Macmillan, 1960.

Steiner, Rudolf. *Esoteric Development: Selected Lectures and Writings from the Work of Rudolf Steiner*. Spring Valley, NY: Anthroposophic Press, 1982.

—. *Evolution of Consciousness*. Trans. V. E. Watkin and C. Davy. Sussex: Rudolf Steiner Press, 1991.

—. *How Can Mankind Find the Christ Again?* Hudson, NY: Anthroposophic Press, 1984.

—. *Karmic Relationships*. Trans. George Adams. Vol. 1. Letchworth, GB: Rudolf Steiner Press, 1972. 8 vols.

—. *Occult Science*. 1920. Trans. Maud and Henry Monges. Spring Valley, NY: Anthroposophic Press, 1972.

—. *Rudolf Steiner: An Autobiography*. Trans. Rita Stebbing. Blauveldt, NY: Rudolf Steiner Publications, 1977.

—. *The Search for the New Isis, Divine Sophia*. Spring Valley, NY: Mercury Press, 1983.

Stephen, Leslie. *Hours in a Library*. 1876. London: John Murray, 1920. 3 vols.

Sturrock, J. "Wordsworth and Vaughan." *Notes and Queries* 24 (1977): 322-23.

Swift, Jonathan. *Gulliver's Travels*. Ed. Paul Turner. Oxford: Oxford UP, 1986.

Taylor, Anya. "Religious Readings of the Immortality Ode." *SEL* 26 (1986): 633-54.

Trilling, Lionel. "Wordsworth's Ode: Intimations of Immortality." In *The Liberal Imagination*. New York: Viking, 1950, 124-54.

Vendler, Helen. "Lionel Trilling and the Immortality Ode." *Salmagundi* 41 (1978): 66-86.

Willey, Basil. *The Eighteenth-Century Background: Studies on the Idea of Nature in the Thought of the Period*. London: Penguin, 1962.

Wimsatt, W. K., and Monroe Beardsley. "The Intentional Fallacy." 1933. In *Critical Theory Since Plato*. Ed. Hazard Adams. Rev. ed. Orlando: Harcourt Brace Jovanovich, 1992, 944-51.

Wöhrer, Franz K. *Thomas Traherne: The Growth of a Mystic's Mind*. Elizabethan and Renaissance Studies Series 92:6. Gen. ed. James Hogg. Salzburg: Institut für Anglisitik und Amerikanistik, 1982.

Wordsworth, Christopher. *Memoirs of William Wordsworth*. Ed. Henry Reed. 2 vols. Boston: Ticknor, Reed, and Fields, 1851.

Wu, Duncan. *Wordsworth's Reading, 1770-1799*. Cambridge; New York: Cambridge UP, 1993.

—. *Wordsworth's Reading, 1800-1815*. Cambridge; New York: Cambridge UP, 1995.

Yates, Christine. *Brother Klaus: Man of Two Worlds*. York: W. Sessions, 1989.

Index

0-595-22444-X